Snippets of Ink

By Joshua Crocker

SNIPPETS OF INK

979-8-9879131-1-6 (paperback)

Library of Congress Control Number: 2023904895

Cover design by Joshua Crocker.

Photos taken by Joshua Crocker.

Classic version, paperback print. First edition 2023.

Published by the Paragon Coalition.
Norman, OK
paragoncoalition.com

Dedicated to...

The pen on my chest,
my best friend even
in the weirdest of times.

Introduction *by Joshua Crocker*

Why read when you can write? Why laugh when you can sing? Why sit still when you can run? Where are you going? Who are you right now?

Grab a pen, this book is already filled with ink-stained pages, who cares if you add a few more. As you're reading, write down your own thoughts. Make notes of the words that mean something to you, add a star to your favorite pages so you don't forget where to find them. Make each chapter of this book yours, make each copy of this book unique. Each person reads different, they'll find something special about the words they're reading that no one else does. They'll take what the author wrote and discard it for something better, a snippet of their own life.

I keep writing, each drop of ink something special to me. I took the words I've written and spilled them across these pages. These poems taken from my notebook, the songs I've written, and projects I'm still crafting. Ink and scribbles, pictures scattered across the pages to give a snapshot of what I see in my world.

All words are made up, that's why they make something so powerful.

Table of Contents

Chapter I: I broke my pen

Damn. My pen just broke,
and ink is spilling everywhere.
My thoughts spewing anywhere,
staining my clothes and notebook.

Ink Splashes

The ink splashes on the page
because my art, it's a getaway.
My thoughts become words
because the pen, it's a gateway.

I Can Write, But I Can't Sing

Ring, ring, ring!
I can write, but I can't sing.
La-la-la-la-la-la-la!
No one wants to hear what was just sung,
the words get caught on my tongue,
roll off like a klutzy toddler on a diving board.
I just want to say what's on my mind
but I'm better with the pencil than the guitar.
So, if this song sounds bizarre
just remember, I can write, but I can't sing.
La-la-la, la-la-la, la-la-laaaa.

Pen Name

Maybe I should write under a pen name?
I could call myself Levithan Lynx.
Maybe that's too mystical though.
I'm just afraid that when people
find out who I really am,
they won't like the real me.
I could call myself Joshua Castell.
Close enough, right? Yeah, right.
Without my name out there to shame,
I could write without my fear of rejection.
But I did use a photo of myself on the cover.
I could call myself Auhsoj Rekcorc.
Named after my favorite superhero, action-star.
What if I just attribute these words
to someone else, someone who's not me.
Maybe I should write under a pen name?
But then these words wouldn't be mine.

That Sound

You call me an angsty poet.
You think I don't know it?
Do my words not show it?
I'm the kid ready to blow it all.
An emotional know-it-all.
How's that sound to you now?

Cussing at the Wind

I don't mind blaming it on the rain
and I won't stop cussing at the wind.
I can't wait for Friday,
so I can wish that it were Monday again.

Jesus, Was I Worth It?

I sit alone on a pew at church,
I'm feeling out of it, lonely and stuck.
I've got a lot of questions on my mind,
but I'll trust you in all of it,
yet I still need to know:
Jesus, was I worth it?
Every day I make mistake upon mistake,
I spend more time with my anxiety than you,
do you still feel the nails every time I fail?
I cuss in my songs, but I try so hard to live with love.
I let my pride take over, trying to find faith in myself.
Do you smile knowing when you died it was for me?
Please tell me you do.

Earbuds; Coffee Shop

Monday morning is a highlight of the week for me,
sleep till seven, wake up and eat breakfast,
then I'll head to a coffee shop to write.
I've got a short poem from yesterday to add to my
book, and so many new rhymes echoing in my brain.
I'll put in my earbuds, shuffle a playlist with
Olivia Rodrigo and My Chemical Romance,
because I like to scream when I'm crying.
But I'm writing. So many thoughts,
writing a new melody, discovering a new story.
My earbuds sound out everything around here,
with my variety of music that speaks, at least to me.
A caffeinated sugar high and a keyboard,
a deadly combo for my hyperactive side;
the way I am that I've begun to embrace.
The Monday morning rain showers,
the return to another work week won't bother me,
because I've found a little life
that means something to me.

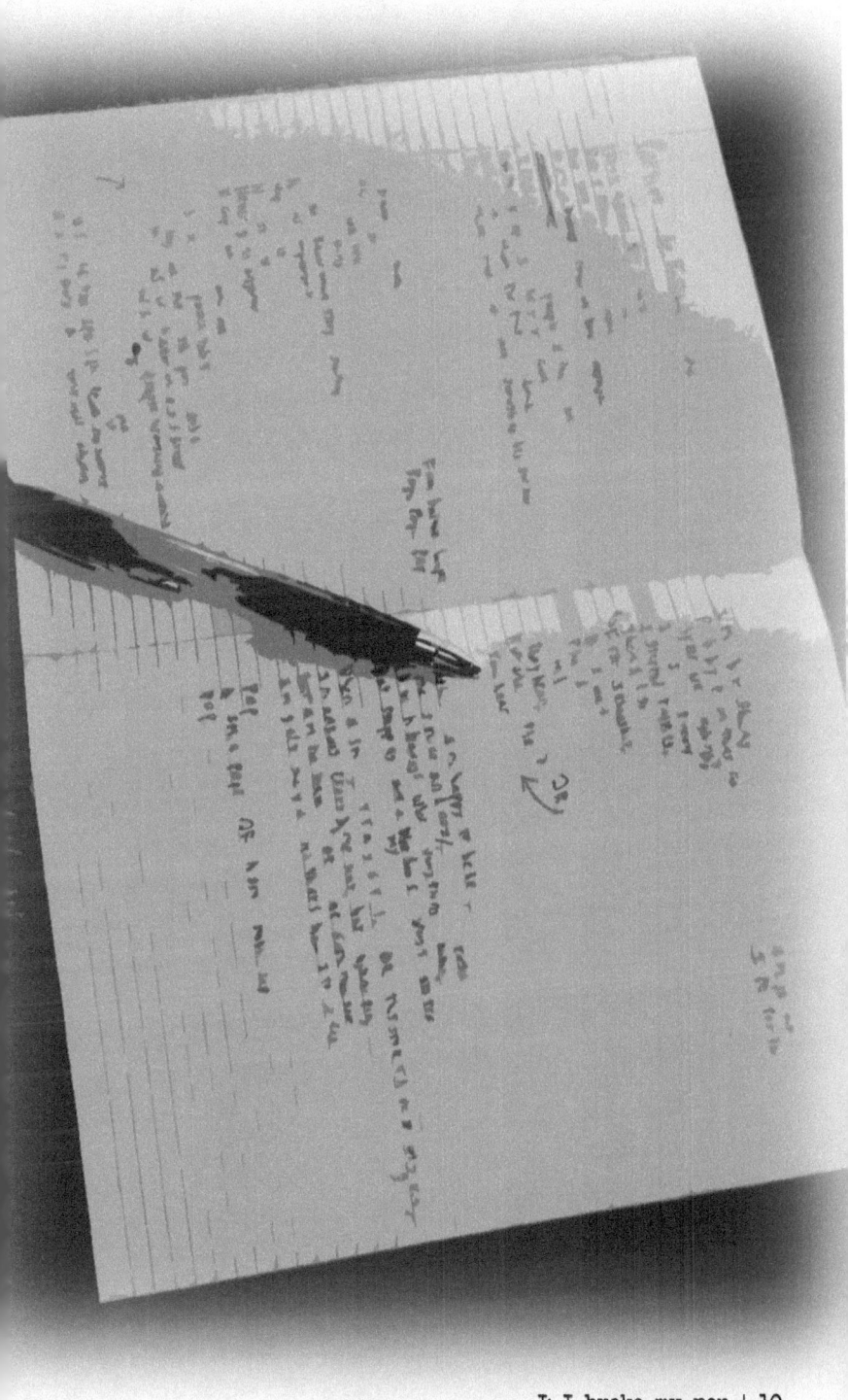

New Spring

It's a new spring, thank you God for loving me every day. I see glory in the colors around me.

Little Extra

Hey, I'm sorry if I seem a little extra,
I get anxious when talking to you,
sometimes I say the weirdest stuff,
but when you leave it's never enough.

Contradiction

Oh, here we go!
I'm stuck inside my head,
can't tell the good from the bad,
can't find the difference between me, myself, and I.
I'm the best at saving my best for later.
Oh, here we go!
I know how this song goes,
this is a contradiction of pride,
time to take a side!

Music Is My Therapy

I prefer living life alone. Ha, and I wonder why I'm so lonely. I won't open up to you because I leave myself vulnerable. The words we say to each other are unalterable. I wasn't lying when I said my biggest fear was the truth.

Music is my therapy. Poems are my counseling. I'm honest with myself, otherwise I wouldn't be writing anymore, so why should I be honest with you?

Champagne Flute

Break the champagne flute,
flip the calendar page.
Under the night sky's bombs
we enter on to a new pier,
the one full of smiling fear
of where we veer and steer.
It's what we see appear
when we hear from our ears,
the joy and hope of a new year.

Rip Away, Next Page

1st: A new start, I can't wait.
2nd: Think of all the great things ahead of me!
3rd: Ooh, shiny.
4th: Wait, it's already the 4th?
5th: I'm hungry, what's for lunch?
6th: This new calendar is pretty cool.
7th: First week down, I got something done at least.
8th: Want to hear a joke?
9th: Anxiety. Haha.
10th: That's it. That's the joke. I'm hilarious.
11th: I should be a writer.
12th: But like, a good one.
13th: Ooh, spooky it's the 13th.
14th: What's really spooky:
15th: The month's already halfway over.
17th: I forgot yesterday's page.
18th: Hope that doesn't happen again.
21st: Shit, I'm behind. And hit snooze.
23rd: Hey, today was a pretty good day.
24th: I'll just do my best today, every day.
25th: And I know my best will just get better.
26th: Well, I'd hope so anyway.
28th: I forgot another page.
29th: Hey, it'll be okay.
30th: I guess this year won't be a perfect one.
31st: But today was a still a good day. Yay. ☺

I Hate School

Hey! Mom and dad are proud!
I got another A on some test,
I didn't really study, why be bothered
when I can pass in record time!
Essays riddled with red marks
but in my poems, I can mispeel all I want!
Probably have an undiagnosed focus disorder,
doodled a map in my brain
and skimmed the page because reading's hard,
I rather listen to music and write!
History and language arts are a waste
when I could be doing karate, hi-ya!
Spent days at the library from K-8th grade,
I was a top student in high school,
and now I'm working on a college degree,
but oh, ya know, I still hate school.
Oh ya know, I hate school.
Oh ya know, I hate school.
This assignment drools,
doodling sports scores rules,
becuz, oh ya know, I hate school!

I'm writing songs instead,
thinking one day I'll know why I'm here.
When I really care about something,
that's when I give it my all,
and this just simply ain't that.
The education of life isn't in a classroom,
a pile of homework, or a meeting on Zoom.
But here I am, and I know I'll give it my best.
Because it feels like my best is all I got.

Hopeless Romantic

Some days I feel like a hopeless romantic. I use poetry to ascribe some sense from the semantic. My words catch up to me; I can write, but I can't sing. It didn't stop me from writing a song to the girl with a pretty face, because I can't get her off my mind. I can hear your infectious laugh through a mask. I wonder if an aurora shines as bright as you. You're weird in the most familiar way, the same way I feel around you. I'll write my thoughts down, so I don't forget what to say.

These Songs and Poems

I'm writing like I'm fighting to stay alive. These songs and poems will be the death of me. And I'm better person thanks to each word. Truly. This romantic season brings each thought to ink. Each leaf a lyric in my life.

this is where I'm at
walking around a maze
looking for you

you're the reason I keep going

I'm not ready to lose this
because if I lose my friends

then I've made it to the end

hey... I wrote something

I wrote it for myself

or well I guess I wrote it for you too

I, uh, do you ever feel lost in your thoughts

um, what was I thinking

do you feel lonely?

not that you're alone
and not that people don't
understand

it's more like, you're stuck in your head

if you read this,

actually on second thought maybe you
shouldn't

or should you?

I just need one more edit...

the key,

the words we read

the words we write

it's the way we are
the ink in every thought
the love in every drop

I wrote something
I hope you read it

I hope you need it

Driving Home I

I enjoy driving with the windows down. I feel so alive when the breeze rushes against my face. Some days I get behind the wheel only to frown. But when I think about today, I know I rather focus on the good over the bad. Every day I live for a promise that will never leave me alone. God, you said you'll always be by my side, and I want you to know for that, I'm glad.

Who I Am

You started writing poetry. Gross.
You told me it was a way to feel free,
I didn't believe you.
I rather write a script for a movie.
You snickered at me and said
I should learn how to write about who I am,
instead of trying to be who I never can be.
I still think about that.

An Excerpt From My Novel:
What Zoey Told Leo

"I've always imagined my life as some sort of science fiction adventure. Every day I look around, hoping to find some mystery to solve. Yet I'm always so hesitant to do anything. I think I might be terrified that I'll just fail. What if I can't handle this? A storm tossing you into the air, secret information, the pressure of feeling alone outside of this house."

"Leo, there are two types of people that never get stories written about them. Like you said, the first one is a failure. But the second one, even worse, is people who don't try anything."

Zoey searched through her bag, pulled out a fountain pen, and handed it to Leo.

"Here, write your own story."

Frauds

I won't trust a writer,
they're paid to make lies sound good.
Poets are melodramatic fools
who try to makes hurricanes out of a little rain.
They're masochists who love pain,
because it gives them something to say.
Writing's not a talent, anyone can do it.
Poets are frauds.
They make art out of nothing at all.

Stained

Damnit, the page is stained.
The keys fall off my typewriter,
the gloves come off the fighter.
"Keep your guard up!" they shout.
Hide my words where the world can't find.
The ink soaks in.
The fear of what I've said,
it makes me doubt who I've become.
I won't fall in love until the moment's perfect.
I won't write without shaking, anxious,
the spill of ink an imperfection.

Write a Poem Chapter I

_____

_____

_____

_____

_____

_____

_____

_____

_____

_____

_____

_____

_____

_____

_____

_____

_____

_____

_____

_____

Chapter II: I'm like the corn in a maze

The fence blocks the path,
and I hear my tormenter laugh.
He knows if I were just a little taller,
then I wouldn't need to find
the bridge to success. But alas.

Cocky Superstar

Oh! Welcome to my life,
my unearned confidence and I
taking center stage.
I'm a cocky superstar
rocking this place!
My inspiration takes me far,
the word hero comes to mind,
the main character in my life's story.
I know I'm great, at least I think I do,
that's what's true and you have no clue.

Center of the World

Hey baby brother, I just gotta ask,
what's going on in your mind?
I'm a hotshot sixteen-year-old
trying to be the center of my world.
You're just a baby staring blankly
living in the center of your world.

ODIK: Internalization

As a kid I loved mazes, cool thing is that's life!
Situations, you wonder about expectations.
Will today be the best day ever?
Because I'm feeling unsure of where I'm going.
You see, ambitious hopes leave you exhausted
and I wonder if I have what it takes to be me.
Am I the best teacher, writer,
or person for to be certain?
Hey, are you ready?
That's the question I keep asking me.
I'm sure one day I'll know.

December Morning

I'm seventeen now. Graduation and New Year's are in sight. That first Christmas you held me; did you imagine how I would turn out? Are you proud of the young man I'm becoming? You raised and cared for me; you woke up early to hide those last presents under the tree. Are you ready for me to start my own life, or are you as terrified as me?

Partner in Crime

Every day a partner in crime,
mix and load a cherry-lime,
rob a bank to find a spare dime,
what other words can I use to rhyme,
because this has always been our time,
so watch out world, because this mime,
he says, "mmm-mmm-mmm."
Soccer, call it football,
snow cones and popsicle sticks,
enough kicks and I'll be sick.

Every night when you fall asleep,
I still walk by and wish you a good night,
say I love you, but y'know,
we're driving in the skyyyyyy,
life is our apple!
We're driving in the sky,
life is our apple pie!

The Six-Point Method

Alright, I got six points for forward thinking:
Mentis – Get smarter and you'll be better off.
Supposedly. I don't care for learning though, so just
skip this part.
Socialis – What are your friendship goals?
For me, it's to have one. I like to set the bar low.
Gloria – You know it's important to clear your
mind and grow internally. Which is why I'm taking
some me-time to browse the internet.
Personalis – What inspires you? For me it's writing,
creating things, and making snarky lists. This area is
for all that, so in my experience just focus all your
energy on whatever shit you want to do and ignore
the other five points.
Corporis – Reminder: Money does buy happiness.
Just saying. So, you probably should just get some.
Phasellus – Now this point has four sub-points:
hygiene *(be attractive)*, fitness *(be fast)*, diet *(learn
to cook, mostly just to impress girls)*, and routine
(wake up early, then immediately get on your phone).
So just memorize and do all of that.

It's my foolproof six-point method!
That has never once worked.

Introversion's Curse

Time by yourself is nice, I'd say.
Introversion's curse is your recursion.
Girls, work, eating, faith, and news.
Sports, numbers, creativity, and you.
It's a bit much to take in, don't you think?
Because you always are. You always are. *Sigh*.

Emotional Variance

My life is going great, and I won't shut up about it. I lose count of everything I'm happy about. Haha, deep down I know I'm a spoiled brat. Ain't that the shit.

But in case you're new to this whole life thing, I'll let you know. Everyday wear comes for free. My sleep schedule is fine except when it isn't. I keep myself busy, because otherwise I just feel tired. Sometimes nothing sounds good, and I don't always eat well. I'll still love you though.

Each Day

Do you know how weird life will be?
You were born a month after an election,
our country tensed up at the reaction.
Your mom's smiling behind a mask,
horror or war, get ready to laugh,
each day will be the best till the last.

Middle American Heroes

We're the upper-lower-middle class types,
the Middle American heroes on the 9 to 5,
driving down the freeway goin' fifty-five.

They told me buy low, sell high,
my friends rather just get high.
They told me all about the good ol' days
but welcome to the present days, (hip-hooray!)
where instead you sell what you got
and buy dirt because you're a filthy dot.
Mud in the air, cracks in the streets.
If we squint past that,
we may just see your make-believe,
and now I see a land of dreams!
Yesterday's future is here! (see!)

Hostile Takeover

This is a hostile takeover!
When the lights go out,
remember who told you to shout.
I'll get rid of all the weight holding us back
and blow up this entire operation!
Grab hold of what your fear,
remember who told you to cheer.
I'm the visionary, creator of problems,
and solver of what your fight.
For tonight I take over and we're
going to start doing things my way.
This is the only way to win,
remember who told you to grin.

Now stand and fight and never run away.

King of the World

Too all my loyal subjects,
what's it like to live in the shadow of greatness?
I can't imagine being as lucky as you,
to have had the honor of meeting me.

Oh-oh-oh, yo!
I'm the king of the world!
The eighth wonder,
the masked crusader.
Cool as fuck, coming in hot,
bask in the greatness, y'all I'm great.
I'm the king of the world!
The damn star of the show,
got the universe circling around me.
I'm the king of the world!

Thinking

Do you really think I'm stupid?
Like I don't know who I am,
because you remind me of every little thing,
I think what you think is enough,
and I've had it with your high and mighty pride.
Guess what kid, you don't know shit, huh!

Why?

Lord, why do my fingers bleed?
Why do I carry these bad habits with me?
Why, when it's your wrists that bleed
and you carried the cross with thee.
Every day I bite away my insecurities,
I think with my brain and die with my heart.
You died on my part,
and found the lost souls that needed a friend.
So why am I still lost?
Why do I feel the need to defend
against every good thing?
I want to see if these fingernails
will take away my anxiety,
even if it causes me to bleed.
Lord, why can't I figure this out?
And why won't I let you do it for me?

this may sound dangerous
but I got to thinking

what if I could write the perfect story?

put a pen in my hand,
put my life in my hands

the pressure

I'll collapse

that voice, it won't go away

but I've begun to tell it to shut up,
I've begun to make friends with it,

I've begun to learn how to trust it

I should go back to writing
superhero movies

because then I can finally be a hero

bridges make me scared,
what if it collapses under me?
what if I collapse under the pressure?

even worse, what if I cross over it?

I don't want to be where I can't see

I don't want to be where I don't have the pen

mightier than the sword

I'm weaker than a sword
though I've been training my kicks and punches for years

what am I afraid of?

why do I let that friend lie to me,
the one in my head,
the one who tells me everyone else
doesn't like me

shut up

bridges,
I can't wait to see what's on the other side

because then I can finally be ordinary
but to me, everything will look like a movie

Don't Mess With the Sun

Don't mess with the sun,
he'll blind us all. Oh, just shine on.
Keep up the mountain view, hide in sight,
I'm looking for something when I'm better at hiding.
Poets are the kings of lying. Oh, just shine on.
I just wanted a hug on a winter night,
she hugged me tight. Oh, just shine on.
I can't see where I'm not going,
I won't find what I'm not looking for.
I just wanted a hug on a winter night,
but I don't have anyone.
Oh, just shine on, won't you shine on.
I can't be what I don't believe in,
I won't need what I never wanted.
I just want a hug. Don't we all.

Take a Walk

When the living room runs out of room
for me to pace around time and time again,
I'll go outside. I'll take a walk.
Music in my left ear and the wind in the right.
Wistful feelings,
wishful breathing.
The water reflects the thought back to me.
My wondering thought loses me,
on the streets of the neighborhood belonging to me.
The red dirt.
The sediment in each sentiment.
The sunset is beautiful. I'll remember it.
Time is a maze when you can't see,
my home is near me.
When I'm lost, I'm finally free.
I'll take a walk and clear my mind.
I'll take a walk and see what I find.

Intentional Retention

I have the intention of retention,
this tension my retrospection.
The circumvention of my attention
for prevention of contention.
Did-idilie-doo.
Why can't you just focus like a normal person?
For the intervention of comprehension
is the mention of my dissention.
My suspension of condescension,
an ascension of apprehension.
Did-idilie-doo.
Why can't you just focus like a normal person?

Shortcut

Based on my stature,
you would think I'm good at taking shortcuts.
And you would be right.
Take the easy path out,
never do anything challenging.
When driving, I know all the backroads to get to
places faster, that my sister swears take longer.
(And technically speaking, she would be correct.)
'Think smarter, not harder' is a mantra I know well.
I bring a rock to a maze of mirrors
and butter to a maze of corn.

My inner voice calls me a quitter and a loser,
but I've got another way of thinking about it.
When I pour my soul into what I care about,
it's doesn't seem hard because it's what I love.
I don't take shortcuts,
just my own path.

December Morning II

Hey mom and dad, thanks. All the presents were nice, but it isn't the unwrapping that I'll remember, but the people smiling this morning in December. You prepared me for the best and I'll be back for the worst. I'm still worried, but you tell me I'll always make you proud and I don't plan on changing that.

Write a Poem Chapter II

Chapter III: I can't find the light switch

Who moved the light switch?
Seriously, I can't see.
Wait, I think I found it.
No, that just... turned the fan on.
Who puts the switch to the fan
on a different wall!?
Y'all.

the dark

i'm still afraid of the dark,
monster eyes peaking from my closet,
quick, turn on the lamp.
i hear a rattle down the hall,
a shake under the bed,
emptiness surrounds me.

I Don't Like Sleep

I don't like sleep
'cuz I'm a hyperactive freak.
I'm afraid of a world where
my thoughts stop flowing,
'cuz then I'll be knowing,
what it's like to be dead.
And for that reason, I won't get in bed
until I got a thought in my head,
like reminiscing something she said,
something to keep me dreaming
of why tomorrow will be great,
even if that's hardly ever the case.

Little White Lies

Your little white lies,
you're the ghost inside my mirror.
Your little white lies,
I'm drowning in my fears.

Your little white lies,
you're the ghost inside my mirror.
Your little white lies,
the whisper in my ears.

Your little white lies,
you're the ghost inside my mirror.
Your little white lies,
the sorrow in my tears.

Your little white lies,
you're the ghost inside my mirror.
Your little white lies,
you're the friend who endears,
the enemy who sneers,
and your voice is always near.

Elevator

What would happen if I got stuck in an elevator
and I couldn't trust in my savior?
I'm talking about me.
What would happen if I couldn't set myself free,
from the broken gears and strings?
If the air in here starts to dissipate,
because I keep breathing in a desperate
attempt to push all the buttons,
then my lungs will begin to claustrophobize.
I guess I'm just gonna die.
Welp, I had an alright run, RIP and bye.

Save Me, I'm Dying

We'll make out under the flickering lights.
When it's just you and me.

Save me, I'm dying.
Save me, I'm dying.
Save me, I'm dying.
Save me, I'm dying.
Save me, I'm dying.

I'll take your heart in a trickling fight.
Now it's just you and me.

Birds and Flowers

Worrying over the birds and flowers,
not trusting in your comfort and power.
You know how I'm anxious and live life in my head,
I try to feel better by taking control.
But in the end, I know I've let myself down more
than anyone else ever could.

What If?

What if I didn't know why I'm here?
If I lost my belief in you, would you cast me away?
What if love and faith are lies?
Is that what being truly lost is like?
What if I wasn't raised in a loving home?
Would I still be sitting here now,
or would I be failure because I couldn't cut it?
I'm not that great, probably just sorta lucky.
What if I waste the next years of my life
for something that doesn't matter?
I'm writing when I should be reading.
I'm talking when I should be listening.
What if I wasn't me?
Who would I be then?

ODIK: Faith

The more my faith grows, it feels like the less I know.
Love unaltered is hardly ever unfaltered.
Am I the one who believes what's wrong?
Because few people share what I see, here and there.
You see, love's been replaced with fear and control
and I wonder if that's truth
or if there's answer in prayer.
How do you trust more in the doubt
than dying in the lying?
Who do I love most?
Me, you, Jesus, or all the above.
I'm sure one day I'll know.

Just Peachy

Oooooh! You better listen up.
You preach love, but all I hear is blah-blah-blah.
You flash your smile and jaw-jaw-jaw. Ha!

Y'all are so preachy that everything is so peachy,
what if we stopped to talk it all out,
maybe instead of crying themselves to sleep,
we could figure out an end to all the doubt.

The Cynical State I

Your teens are crying, nearly dying,
tears covering our bedsheets,
blood under our shirtsleeves.
You wanna know somethin' funny?
When you tell someone they're unloved,
they feel like no one loves them.

The Cynical State II

Mental Health?
Haharhaha, we all knows that's not real.
Just be happy, that's the deal.
I mean sure it'd be easier if things weren't so cynical,
but when the air sucks and bandages are for the rich
your head starts to feel clinical.
So, if you want to play this game, fine.
Let's do it. Let's get political.

Lonely

There's nowhere I feel more lonely than church,
my friends have all left or aren't around,
and I feel different from everyone else.
Too old for the kids, too young to be a man,
too liberal for the conservatives that I don't agree with.
I feel like I don't belong, am I wrong?

Sayin' Nothing

Stand around as we say damn you all to hell,
but we won't say a word about the hell we've made fall.
There's something wrong and we ain't done a thing,
sayin' nothing right now will cause more harm to us all.

Monsters

Those monsters lurk around every corner.
They hide in your closet and under your bed.
They won't say it, but they want you dead.
So don't run and don't scream,
you won't ever want to dream,
they're after you, after you, won't you know.
Daytime is at its darkest at high noon,
when you won't take out your pistol and duel.
The monsters rule, they rule over you, they rule.
Take out your pistol and duel, won't you know.
So don't run and don't dream,
please for the love of me, turn on the light please.
They lurk and lurk and lurk,
under every thought and talk, they talk,
they hide in sight and pull the shades.
When you see red, don't drop dead,
the monsters smell your fear, I said.
Drop dead, don't drop dead, pull the shades,
pull your pistol and duel, today you duel.
Kill the monsters or the monsters will kill you.

Tense

My editor told me to be sure to use the right tense.
I *was* tense in the past.
I *am* tense in the present.
I *will be* tense in the future.

sleep with the lights on

you know why every night i sleep with the lights on?
i happily spend a lot of time by myself,
but being alone scares the shit out of me till dawn.

...
...
...

what is it like to feel sad?

what is it like to die?

what is it like to feel happy?
I think I'm happy
I feel happy

what does it mean to feel something?

what is it like to be alive?

I really do sleep
with a light on

are monsters real?

why do I write about
the same things

I write about spiritual matters like I know
what I'm talking about

I sing about love, I've never been in love

I write about anxiety
but have never met
someone with as much as
confidence as myself

liar

what?

you heard me

I walk a thin line, between the daytime and night sky
wobble   wobble   wobble

don't fall of the fence

wobble

what was it I said that one time

I'm only a kid trying to be a light when it feels dark

it's awfully dark
I guess I need to start smiling

Happiness

I'm still smiling.
You too, yay!
I'm still smiling.
Enjoying this beautiful day!
I'm still smiling.
Because that's what I got to do!
Jostling soda syrup makes me a corporate wizard,
I ain't like my pet lizard,
her cave has a picture of Michelin.
That's the tire guy!
Happiness is a requirement of being sad!
Happiness, yaaayyyyy!

Driving Home II

What if I made a mistake? I've yet to meet anyone a harsher critic of me than me. What if today wasn't perfect, where do I go now? You know me better than any other. When you tell me to trust you, I'll reluctantly reply. I trust you over all else, but I fear losing control. All I know is following you is where I'm going now.

Leave that Doubt

Now don't cry, things can get better,
that's what we're all wondering.
You've got it easy kid,
all I do is worry about the next day,
y'know, whether God made each and every tree,
can I finish the year with all A's,
or if this girl would ever actually like me.
That content look you give me,
it's quite admirable.
Next time I'll try to live in the now,
leave that doubt for tomor-row.

Hey baby brother, I look down at you now,
I think maybe you're just happy being alive.
And y'know, so am I.

The Off Switch

ON
My thoughts are always on.
My mind in a race, going 60 miles per hour.
Sometimes I just wish I could stop always thinking.
Always worrying, always debating myself,
always planning, always berating myself.
Just imagine, a place with no more imagining.
OFF

...

...

...

This sucks.

...

But it's what my worst fear is:
To live without my thoughts.
It's to not be me.
ON
There's no off switch in my head,
honestly, thank goodness.
It's exhausting but fulfilling.
Day or night, I keep the light burning.
I keep the light shining.

Write a Poem

_____

_____

_____

_____

_____

_____

_____

_____

_____

_____

_____

_____

_____

_____

_____

_____

_____

_____

_____

_____

_____

Chapter IV: The sign on the wall says "LVOE"

I apologize for not smiling enough,
when in reality I actually care quite a bit.
Ink is the blood flowing from the heart,
in addition to y'know, actual blood.
What I'm trying to say is, well,
I hope you like this song.

Aurora

All the mysteries of space,
all the questions in the universe,
but I just wonder to myself,
can an aurora shine as bright as you?

Lonely, Wait Actually

I wonder if there's another soul who feels like mine,
if I could find a friend to set this place aflame.
Because of your sacrifice, I know you love me.
I pray to ask you to give me the courage to find
another who needs me to say what I believe,
because this faith should be
about the relationships I've made.

A Love Song to Writing

A paper with a poem is full of life
and is an endless esse of emotion.
The heart is kind and love,
the dove is peace from above.
Fires of sin and the angered wrath,
the searching on his never-ending path.

Chess Game

I love people and the friends I have,
which is why I'm so scared to talk to them.
An introvert with social skills
and a healthy amount of anxiety
is like making a chess game
out of chutes and ladders.

Where I Sit

There's this trend I've noticed since middle school,
wherever I sit, is where everyone else isn't,
and I'm kinda okay with that. Mostly...
it sure is less scary than talking to people,
but I still feel left out when I hear all the chatter,
wondering if I were sitting with them,
maybe I could talk myself into fitting right in.

Broadway Star

I'm singing in the shower,
the star of my Broadway musical.
Every conversation goes the perfect way,
the way they'd never go if I sung what to say.
Hey!

Do You Like Me?

Do you like me?
Because right now I'm not sure you do.
Tell me all the great things,
which I don't believe.
Do you like me?
Cuz, I'm waiting for you to say so.

                                        is love earned?

the pain in my chest

                    the rain in my eyes

            makes me feel alive again
            makes me want to run away again

                                    I'm the most confident,
                                    anxious person I know

            a quick glance,
            what is it about you?
                                I can't take my eyes of you

but every song I write is the same,
        boy meets girl and falls for her,
                but his own insecurities keep him
                        from telling her how beautiful she is to him

            and here I am

                    in the same coffee shop

                            the one with the sign

                thinking about you
                thinking about the night we
                grabbed a drink with friends

                thinking about what to say next time we speak

                                        my writing is a
                                  remix of my emotions

does everyone think their friends find them an inconvenience?
          like a people-watching evening,
                    maybe I can finally talk
                    myself into fitting in

can I play a key change in my music?
I can't even play three chords,
I can't even sing without emotion taking over
can I play a key change in who I am?

                    maybe take the good parts of me
                    and live without fear of heartbreak

after all,
mom and dad still love you
                              even though they live on
                              different streets

          if I can just make everyone happy we'll be okay,
          but she's the one who makes me smile,
          every time she looks my way

          if I can make people laugh,
          maybe I won't see another friend's bloody arms
          or have to get another call that you almost died

          if I can let someone else feel loved,
          maybe then they'll love me

Suicide Notes and Divorce Papers

I strongly believed a piece of paper is freeing,
writing one of the best things you can do.
But words are powerful.
To be honest, words scare me.
I was thinking about why it's so important to me,
to make sure everyone feels like they belong.
Why did I write a song?
Was it about love all along?
Be careful with the words you say.
Not everything written down will free us.
I write to erase the pain from words and thoughts
that would otherwise take us away.
I won't give up, not until everyone I love has a smile.
And I very well may die trying.
But I love you all, no matter the pain.

Wedding Cake

What the fuck!
Wedding cake is a scam.
It's just fancy vanilla that costs twice as much,
just because it's all lovey-dovey!
You know what: Love is a scam.
Now hear me out,
I could go have a nice dinner by myself,
or I could pay twice as much just to stare
awkwardly at someone as they eat.
Wow, what a great deal, he said sarcastically.
Flowers give florists financial power,
cause I'm pretty sure I can pick flowers for free,
but they charge me this "love" fee.
You think I can afford to be in love?
In this economy! Ha.
I might as well take out a mortgage
any time I flirt with that cute biology major.

And don't even get me started on having kids.
Childbirth, more like grand theft robbery.

Lovesick

This is infuriating the way I feel.
Whenever I see you my stomach drops,
I'm lovesick to my gut, taking tums doesn't help.
It's an illness to feel this; my head hurts,
butterflies in my stomach, why am I like this?

I Can't Get You Off My Mind

Hey, I like you. I really do.
I wasn't sure at first, but now I know it's true.
I've always thought you were kinda cute
and y'know, lately I can't take my eyes off you.
You're the song stuck in my head
when I'm walking at night listening to sappy music.
Your voice echoes through my thoughts
and y'know, I can't get you off my mind.

You're the song stuck in my head,
the one with my favorite rhythm
that I hum along too all the time,
with these poorly written lyrics of mine
about how I can't get you off my mind.

Thoughts to Myself

I'm sorry that I'm keeping my thoughts to myself. You deserve me being honest with you. I'm sorry that I don't have it figured out. The tendencies in me tell me to be an anxious, perfectionist, hopeless romantic. I'm so worried about little things that don't matter and making sure what I write down is the perfect story, when I don't care about any of that. I just want to put my arm around you and talk about whatever, it really doesn't matter if you're smiling up at me.

These are my thoughts written down, when I see you next, I'll tell them to you.

The Song You'll Never Hear

It's the song you'll never hear.
If only I had the courage,
the courage to tell you how I feel.
All the things I would sing during the chorus:
I'd let you know how pretty I find you,
how every damn thing you say makes me smile,
when you're around every problem goes away.

A Pointless Story

Dear you-know-who,
we haven't talked in a year.
You were in this dream I had last night.
Although this dream also had a bunch of marbles
racing in an urchin-filled swamp. And a rock concert.
I wouldn't read into it too much.

Is it weird I still think about you?
I don't miss you.
I don't regret anything, not anymore.
I guess I just think it would be cool
if I could say hi to you again one day.
But if I don't get to, so be it.

I hope you're doing good.
You're in first year of school, I wish you the best.
You're family has been in my thoughts.
(But that's a story for another time.)
I have no clue if you're still dating that guy,
either way I hope you find a boy who will love you.
(Or girl. Is it strange I thought you were gay at one point?)

Oh, and I'm sorry for writing a song
where I said you should fuck off.
I've grown a lot since then.
And you're part of the reason why. Thank you.

Fucking Pink Fairies Everywhere

The last time a girl told me "I love you" she was high,
and I was miserable and depressed. *Sigh*
I went to the mats and kept punching
till my knuckles bled.
If only it could take away the pain for a second.

Lovesick II

Here I am, looking for her in a crowd,
tapping my foot, wishing my thoughts weren't so loud.
I'm sick of all this fake infatuation and crushes,
I wanna have the feeling you get from the rushes
of writing a love song to the girl by your side,
not a letter to my own overthinking, anxious lies.

Donuts on a Bench

We could meet for breakfast,
eat donuts on a bench.
Or if you wanted to sleep in,
we could wait till the sun's awake
then grab coffee and take a walk.
Tonight we could get something to eat,
and go do whatever people do on a Saturday night.
I normally just stay at home and watch cartoons,
so that's always an option as well.
There's so much to do,
and I just want to do it with you.

A Family Living Love

The sign says a Family Living Love.
See what kind of love the Father has given to us.
See what kind of love our family gives back.
We scream and hate, we laugh and frown,
and we still sit proudly on Gospel pews.
Are we a family or a religious mafia team?
Love is patient and kind;
love does not envy or boast;
love is not arrogant or rude.
Everyday show the love,
the love that will make a family of us.

Next to Me

I normally sit toward the end, just a little alone
because people make me nervous.
And that's when you sit down next to me.
I can feel my anxiety laughing at me
as I overanalyze every little move.
I catch the scent of you
as I glance over just to look at you.
Your singing makes me wish I was a better singer,
or at least a better writer so I could impress you.
I fidget with my pen thinking about which
words to write in this short poem about you.
You sit next to me and it's all I can think about.
I should tell her I like the flowers on her book.

Do ~~You~~ I Like Me?

These questions may sound stupid
but deep down I know they're not for you.
Why do you think I need reassurance from you,
unless I wasn't so sure if my words are true?
Do I like myself, is what I really want to know.
Unearned confidence is a mask
for thoughts I keep saying aren't a low.

Do you like me?
Because everything you say tells me you do.
You tell me these great things,
why don't I believe you?
Do you like me?
Because I'm not so sure if I do.

Let Go and Party

Smile,
no more denial,
people lie too,
you're in your head,
be in this place.
Let's go to the party.
Let go and party.
All they want is to be liked by you
and that's what you want too.
Smile. And breath.
Pop. The last balloon drops.
See you soon, :)

Sunspot Freckles

I gaze at your sunspot freckles,
you have the beauty of a spectacle,
your dress as lovely as a solar flare.
No one else radiates like you.

All the wonders of the spectrum
reflect off your beautiful hair.
Your voice resounds a calming hum
and when you smile, I know you care.

Evening Stars

It was late and they had just left the land of stars
but right now all they could see were the evening stars.
The two in the backseat were fast asleep
but a man and a girl in the front seat kept talking.
I'll leave the details of their
conversation for you to estimate,
what they said was genuine, sweet, and intimate.
Under the night sky and beam of car headlights
they said, "I love you," for the first time.

Write a Poem Chapter IV

Chapter V: I used to be afraid of fire, now I'm an arsonist

Hahaha.
I see this vision of watching it all burn,
I had a nightmare of my town up in flames,
I have this idea of smelling the smoke,
and I dream of being the one holding the match.

Bye, Bye

Graffiti runs down my teary face,
what have you done to me?
Who are we, you fool, would you know who?
Vandals of the night, sinners in our eyes,
you're you is what belongs to who.
Who is we, love is high, your end is nigh.
Captives in a hellscape,
your mind trying to escape,
your body dwelling further in mistake.

Bye, hell comes at the end.
Bye, hell comes my friend.

Paragon

Deep in the dark alleys of injustice,
stood a hero none like any other.
Metaphorically speaking he
was a shining light in the dark,
allegorically speaking he
wore all black and was filled with snark.
He would carry a heavy legacy with him thereon,
a superhero, they called him Paragon.

some nights

some nights i decide to be a hero in skies higher,
some evenings i'm a disastrous lovesick villain,
it's a story of where i hope with a voice of desire.

Evangeli$m

You've blurred the line between
evangelism and conservatism,
a capitalist empire is your lovely idea,
say commercialism, an economic ideal
based off men's desire for money,
excuse me honey, but that seems quite contrary,
for the love of money is the root of evil,
I mean it says so in your Bible, check 1 Timothy.
Did you know the early Christian folk shared,
I remember back in pre-k learning that feat,
but hey, you've rebranded it as the dastardly socialism.
You do realize just because faith is a thing,
doesn't require you to abandon logicism.

Shooting Range

Camouflage your insecurities.
I'm afraid of what I don't know,
I carry a gun, afraid I'll become the villain.
My hands are shaky,
my magazine unloaded; bullets unknown.
My pill bottle empty, but I'm the hero.
Right?
The world is my shooting range,
the gunshot ringing in my ears.
The fear dwelling inside of me,
the gunshot deafening me.
I'm the hero. The good guy with a gun.
But... my nights are restless.
Because blood follows me everywhere I go.

The Game

Fairness is no real state.
Tickets for those who can afford the tapering,
play the game and lose to fate,
or be the lucky victor, who all with hate.
I said play the game.
You have no choice.
I said play the game.
This is your fate.
I said play the game.
You have no choice.
Three balls, win the stuffed bear.
One trigger, all here will fear.

Trigger Happy :)

It's not a hate crime when you hate everyone.
If you don't shut up, you'll...
What am I doing? Let me turn on the TV-
Wait, what did they say?!
I'm watching the news, I can feel the fear.
The drugs are wearing off,
I've got these bloodshot eyes,
I think it's time for some bloodshot skies.

In my last moment I'll be a hero,
'cuz I'll be the one to down this zero.
Open the bottle of pills,
oops, looks like I'm out of medication.
Ha-ha-ha, this should be fun.
Load the magazine!
I've got the bullets baby!
The kick back will kill the shitbag.
You think I should walk away from this ledge,
I'll show you what it's like to walk away dead!

punch me, please

a bruised rib is nothing to a broken heart to be reckoned.
i rather get punched in the face ten times
than be left alone with my thoughts for a second.

that calling

talk in riddles
sing with a growl in your voice

it won't
go away

we all will die
you will die

dragon breath, fire's best
blood is currency my dear,
I will drown you in my tears

that calling

it tells me the
flame is the
way

hahwahahahwaha

ink-stained

heartache

the calling
children die for our amusement   it's laughing

I'll die any moment

racket   fuck you!
matches   listen the fuck up!
hatches   I spit on you
heart's aflame   I rule over you
remember my name   I'll fucking end you

the societal norm is found about now

the suicidal norm is killing our nation now

hahwahahahwaha

~~love your enemies and pray for those who persecute you~~

I'll cut off all your enemies from before you
I will make for you a great name

hey, punk   the glistening of a candle

            I have faith until the end
                              you can't handle
        and my end is near

                                     the calling
hey, punk!   is enchanting

                    hahwahahahwaha

            I'm everything you fear!
            self-obsessed
haha   my friends are depressed
            I fucking swear
haha   and simply can't care

        when the world is up in flames,
                    I'm laughing   haha

    I can't wait to burn it all away
            I thought I was writing about my life,
            telling the story from the hero's perspective

no   I'm the villain

                              burn it all
                    flames will cleanse us all
                sinners die in a fiery pit tonight
. b. . .y . .e

                    hahwahahahwaha

Rebel Kids

Meet the rebel kids,
the bastards left behind!
Oh-woo, let's go!
They've got grenades and graffiti,
neo-extremists blowing shit up!
They're agnostic and queer,
everything you fear!
Oh-woo, let's go!

Your sweet upbringing,
the harbinger of chaos in war grounds.
Rebels kids are playing with matches,
they're playing with drugs and pornography,
They're done acting nice,
watch 'em kill you with words,
rebels kids are playing with matches,
try burning a witch with fire,
she'll just cackle at your hellraising.

Shame, shame, shame, shame, shame!
Rebel kids in hoodies,
teens leave blood, let's go!
Watch them burn you all!

Ashamed

How could you do this?
You're better than this.
When everyone hears about what you did,
just imagine what they'll say!
I won't even be able to talk to my friends,
I'll be too embarrassed because of what you did.
You can't just say whatever you want.
You can't just do whatever pleases you.
Your body is temple; would you defile a temple?
Do you feel no shame?

...

Are you crying?
Well I hope so, because this is serious.
I can't believe you would act this way.
You should be ashamed.

Lying Berries

The kids are too smart for their own good,
if they want to learn something,
we'll teach them a lesson:
Burn the books!
Education is the enemy of obedience.
Burn 'em to a crisp.
Step out of line and get shot,
wear the wrong colored clothes
and you'll see what happens slut!
Burn the books!
Education is the enemy of obedience.
Teach a kid what to think and loyalty's yours.
Teach a kid to read...
and you'll have an enemy for life.
Burn the books. Burn 'em good.

Welcome Back

Welcome back to a punk anthem
about those maggots in Washington!
They can't hack it,
they go home crying to mommy,
they live in a broken house
where they can't even unite to pick a speaker.

Welcome back! My voice is shouting!
I'm shouting louder, drown out the
sounds of a whitewashed Christian nation,
killing us in the working class with inflation.
My last chapter was about love,
this one is about the same,
but you need a better aim.
Addition, subtraction of wealth,
multiplication, sociopolitical division.
What's left? This isn't right.

Welcome back! My voice is shouting!
Eyeliner glistening, poster board drying,
a youth revolt, protest incoming.
Stand up for what you believe in.
Stand up for those who believe in you.
Stand up for a faith that will heal us all in time.
Just don't sit down.

The Kids Are Our Future

Hear this: They don't care about us!
"The kids are our future" bullshit
they spout is empty rhetoric.
Stop taking money from our school's piggy bank,
and give me my books back, you hack.
They'll take your rights,
redefine love as their control,
and leave you shackled in your own body.
We can't let them win, vote and protest,
don't boast this, because they don't love us.
The bastards from mommy and daddy's generation
only love their pocketbook.

Redefine

A lot's on my mind a lot. My faith is made a mockery
by the people who taught it to me. I grew up in a day
where I had to learn to think outside the lines and
redefine the world around me. Nothing should scare
you like someone who speaks their mind.

Bleed Out I

The people scream and shout:
Bleed out! Bleed out!
No one to hear you call out!
A wife lies on her deathbed,
her husband doing what it takes to save her.
In desperation he asks his pastor,
he just tells 'em to pray, like they haven't tried that.
Bleed out! Bleed out!
Remember, this is what freedom is now.
The laws the Christians passed
say her life ain't worth it. So just bleed out.

Bleed Out II

He watches his wife sleep.
A break from her misery.
Because of what a few rich hypocrites decided,
she didn't have a choice to die or live.
The men in charge told her sorry,
but she couldn't just do whatever with her body.
There are rules. That they made up of course.
After all if she isn't increasing the populate,
to them what even is her purpose?

A man holds the hand of his love.
She's not sure if she'll make it.
Imagine it, your life-saving medicine just out of reach.
Bleed out.
Remember, this is what freedom is now.
Bleed out.
Christians, why aren't there lives worth it?
Now they just bleed out.

The Trouble Is

Y'know this is all real troublin',
everything seems to be bubblin',
when all's gone to shit, we won't stand tall,
this trouble's here and all of us just stall,
we won't say things or do the what be done,
and that right there is what the trouble is.

Act Like It

It's as simple as 1, 2, forget the 3,
love thy neighbor as yourself.
But you don't act like it,
oh-no, you just don't act like it. Act like it.
You just don't act like it. Act like it.
Oh! Act like it. Act like it.

Newton's Third Law

You may already know him.
It's my old friend,
the consequences of my own actions.

I won't rest until justice is wrought,
and I can get away with shit without
dealing with what all these consequences brought.

Newton said for every action
there is an equal and opposite reaction.
In response I have come to the conclusion:
screw that.

Upside-Down

You're exactly who your parents said you'd be.
Y'know, I stood up for you when no one else did,
look where that got me.
It turns out everyone was right about you,
you're livin' the cliché stereotype,
life turned upside-down, deal with the hype!
You're a selfish motherfucker,
look where that got you.

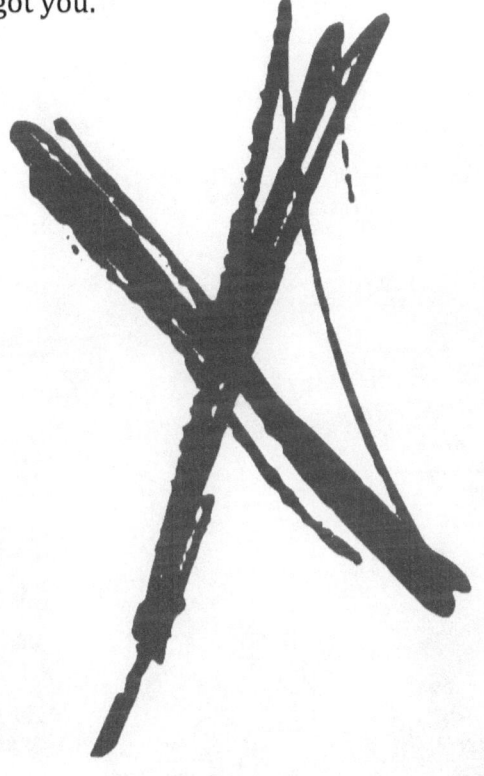

night again

when the days done stars shine at last,
just me and my thoughts are left.
there's nothing that terrifies me like that.

when night falls i'm left alone,
my thoughts echo through my brain,
stuck in a maze; my time to atone.

Call Me Desire

Last call, so you better stop running.
This is it, the greatness haunting you is ahead.
You have 999 voices in your head,
where's the room for me?

You foolish mortals can't see the greatness!
It's right in front of you, it makes me sick.
No more telling me to shut up, you prick!
I'm taking control tonight.
Mr. Misery, the ringing voice in your head,
call me Desire dear.

Drown Kid

Water and fire mix and switch,
don't mind my sinking dear.
I'll ignite and burn out like a star in time.

I was the kid who took off his life vest
and went into the pool again.
Submerged, began to drown.
I don't know how to swim.
Someone saved me (thank you), I don't know who,
but now I won't take the life vest off.
I wade in shallow end, swim where I can't sink.

I burn my past until any manifestation of fear pass.
Afraid of fire, would hide from the flame.
Afraid of everything I know going up in smoke,
I wear a life vest so I can't sink,
run and hide from the heat and my internal defeat.

I'm older now. I'm still the same now.
Walking in the middle of a bridge so I don't fall off.
But no, lose the fear.
It's time to drown kid, take off the life vest,
and be the flame who burns bright into the night.

Good

I'm the good guy with a smile and Bible,
who wrote the song *Goodnight* for goodness' sake.
If broken people try to be better
they're admitting failure before they begin.
Am I a good person or good at justification?

Goodnight

For fuck's sake,
I keep making these mistakes!
It's the same shit,
week in, week out,
I'm getting sick of it!

I keep telling myself there's a next time,
well for the first time can there be a this time.

For fuck's sake,
I keep making these mistakes!
It's the same shit,
week in, week out,
I'm getting sick of it!

ODIK: Society

This, that, be the change you want to see in the world.
Transformation is just new ways of frustration.
Is change ever actually real?
Because there is still hate, poverty, and war.
You see, the people in charge just don't care
and I wonder if I even care enough to fight it.
How do you make a difference
when enough of this is real tough?
Is there any hope?
I'm going to keep trying anyway.
I'm sure one day I'll know.

Church and State

Oh-oh-oh!
It's the separation of church and state,
the expiration of control and hate.
Lies and fear are weapons here.
Oh-oh-oh!
It's our respiration of a heartbeat,
the desperation in my song beat.
Love is the bullet in your mirror.
Bssh-t-t-t-chk!

Ba-ba-bang!
Hear that now!
It's the gunshot of love and peace!
Hide! This is our exasperation of control and hate!
It's the damnation of church and state!

Down in Flames

"Rebel kids are playing with matches."

Smell the smoke.
Watch the world burn.
...
...
Smell the fear.
Watch the world burn.
...
...
Smell the hate.
Watch the world burn.
...
...
...
...
...
The child who is not embraced by the village
will burn it down to feel its warmth.
Everything's about to go down in flames.

Write a Poem Chapter V

Chapter VI: Why can't a tree hug me?

Have you ever hugged a tree?
You just wanted to love something
so desperately you held on a second longer.
The leaves swayed stoutly, confidently.
The tree waits joyfully for rain,
while you're afraid no one needs you.
Now when it rains, you laugh.
You give what you love, no,
you're too afraid of the loss.

I Knew Spring

It's a new spring, and the world feels alright. Me and the birds will sing, and I'll dance in a park at night. I'm driving in the rain with my brand new eyes. The trees shout all that's green, my favorite color to see. I'm back to dreaming of watching the sunset, just that girl and me. I'd be a fool to put it all in words, dare you do the impossible to describe a feeling. A smile on my face and a beat in my heart because I knew spring.

Hair

I play with my own hair,
twirl it around and straighten it out.
I'm a bit nervous, but I usually am.
Honestly most of the time it keeps me in check.
After all, anxiety isn't all that bad.

It's just when I think about it too much.
I think about the last time
I didn't need to mess with my hair,
because I had someone else nearby.
But that's okay, I'm caring for myself right now.
Haha, it doesn't feel like enough does it.

I'm okay with being okay.
I'm happy to play with my own hair,
and take care of myself.
I'm okay with being anxious,
I just wish I stopped letting it be the
rope holding me back,
and instead could let it be the
lasso I use to grab hold of my life.

High Notes and Low Notes

The one thing I know about me
is that I have no clue who I am.
I think I'm the hero of the story
but I contradict it with worry.
So when I switch between
the high notes and low notes,
don't hold your breath.

Day Planner

This is my day planner.
The way I see the world.
I'm driving while thinking.
I'm more focused on what I'll do next,
then where I'm going right now.

My Imagination; An Annoyance

I keep my eyes on the sky,
to see what I know as God's glory.
In the back of my mind,
I know I wish she was by my side.
But I've been getting so sick of my imagination.
Storytelling turns to lies,
when you know it isn't true.

Anecdotal

I like anecdotes.
Just the other day I was boring someone
with a story about my last trip to the store.
I'll tell you about my lunch as if either of us care.
I like telling stories,
but most of them don't mean anything.
The best ones are forgotten to my brain.
Although that does remind me about
that time I saw a squirrel,
which was funny because I literally was just talking
to a different friend about squirrels.
I like telling jokes,
but sarcasm doesn't always land,
and I'm not really that funny,
at best I'm awkwardly clever.
Anyway, I'm getting kind of hungry.
You see, most evenings I get off late,
so I eat dinner after nine and...
Why are you yawning?
Did you not sleep well? I did. I slept great.
When I woke up I thought I heard thunder,
but I was wrong. It was just a truck.
Or the thunder and rain white noise I had playing.
Hey, that reminds me, I was taking a walk
the other day and you'll never believe what I saw...

| Soldiers Run. by Joshua Crocker

Land of the Free

Welcome to the land of the free,
where every week we shop for a
buy three, get one free.
Pollution is our solution,
inflation our incarceration,
but it's the perfect home for me.
This is a tribute to the great folks
of the suburban dream.
God bless Middle America!

Tornado Alley

Tornado Alley tossed the worst at them,
they missed the warning and were driving
towards the twister, now mister,
if you find yourself in a blister, don't resist her.
The storm shook them, rain pouring down,
debris soaring around.
For a second they thought they were going to die,
this was it, the cruel end to a cruel life,
no time for goodbye.
Then they saw the light,
unsure if it was Heaven or lightning-lit skies.
They took a deep breath
and realized they had made it out,
the sun peaked out from behind the clouds' clout,
it was beautiful... but only for a moment.
They were about to find out this was no Heaven,
this was Oklahoma.

Oooaak-la-homa!

The wind came sweepin' down the plain
in Oooaak-la-homa!
The places there were as plain as a coma.
They made their way to the state's center,
there they found a pretty okay city,
the people there were drear nobodies
that anyone would pity;
sad hicks who couldn't put up a fight,
they left that place without
finding a hero or artist in sight.

The Wind

Shuffle the deck for me,
then deal them out face down,
because I keep my cards close to my chest.
I plan my next move here tonight,
I'll strategize what's right.
Don't let the wind take that away.

Opportunity comes a rollin',
I hear a knock at the door,
I'm afraid to go outside,
because the wind might take it away.
I don't want to win if I might lose.
It's the game I'm playing,
the irony is you see...
I always lose anyway.

Hey, Baby Brother

Hey baby brother, I just gotta ask,
what's going on in your mind?
I mean, my head's like a rollercoaster,
a maze with no door to find.
But you stare up at me, just a calm look in your eyes.
I make faces down at you and see your smile light up.
Now I wonder what makes you tick,
all I do is worry about the next day,
y'know, whether God made each and every tree,
can I finish the year with all A's,
or if this girl would ever actually like me.
But you stare up at me, just a calm look in your eyes.
Now I wonder what makes you tick,
I think maybe you're just happy being alive.

Why Do We Worry?

When we have the beauty of the trees.
When your family loves you.
When writing can free you from your chains.
When you find the truth in who you are.
When the peace from sacrifice sets in.
Why?

24-Hour News Cycle

One to twelve, stay tuned for our next story!
All you can do is feel the worry,
if the world never stops around you.
When sadness makes money, all you want is a hug.
But don't give into the temptation!
Research shows hugs are the leading cause
of disease in ages infant to seniors.
One to twelve, keep the TV on,
keep your phone near you;
death, war, famine, conquest, the apocalypse,
and how it affects you! More on this at ten.
If it ever ended you'd be forced to see
your reflection in the motionless screen,
that's what makes me want to scream. Uaagghh!
One to twelve, fear sells. Unplug only if you dare.
The beauty of the trees swaying in spring will be
forgotten in this endless whirlpool of despair.

Who's Who

I'm sure you've heard it all before,
I hardly recognize you anymore.
And I'm not about to mince by words,
we're in this game of who's who
and I'm still playing not to lose,
now I ask you this: How about you?

Stolen Identity

Welcome to a modern day identity crisis.
I'm living my life with a stolen identity,
a failure in the making, you can watch out
when this life I live is up for the taking.
A morally illiterate society is here.
Prove it. Please. Prove it to me.
How can you and I read the same thing
but not see the same words?
So now there is a division of identity.
I fear a revision of complacency,
when we hate our gay brother
and disown our trans sister.
I go to church and hear we've lost our identity.
No, they found who they are.
You just won't look for them.
Remember when you found who you are?
Those waters that changed you. Saved you.
Is your chapel a broken home
or a pearly white country club?
Let me ask, who stole your identity?

Religion Undefiled

What about us: the everyday family?
You're against abortion
and all for family supportion,
but only when dad's at work
and mom's in the kitchen will it work.
The rest of us are struggling
in our broken homes with single parents
or our two moms we can't talk about.
You only care about kids before they're born
or when they're sitting in your class indoctrination.
You take from the poor to give to the rich
for your fixed system of class incongruity.
Instead of fixing the problem
you're taking away the solution.
For James 1:26-2:13,
bridle the tongue, religion undefiled:
visit the orphans and widows,
partiality our sin, for a gold ring ain't better,
don't disregard the poor,
after all the rich disregard you,
mercy triumphs over judgement too.

The World I Know

I was born in '04, never saw the towers fall.
The world I know isn't the
world they show on TV.
The streets are littered with trash,
and our government seats,
also littered with trash.
They won't let teachers or kids go to school
if they might learn something.
They won't help us,
so it's about time we help ourselves.
If they suspend us for looking out
for our friends who are different,
then we'll picket the schoolyard
and remind 'em why they fear us.
The world is filled with hate and panic,
and we've felt it since birth.
They may not thank us, but we'll be the ones
who will put an end to it.

Deodorant

Hi! Quick life lesson,
if you're going to give people a hug,
wear deodorant.
And if you want someone to hug you,
you better be prepared to hug them too.

I've been spending all my time trying to escape

worried about a world I have no control over

when I could instead write the story
with the pen in my hands

I take pride in my creativity

from a young age I wrote lists and maps
to make some semblance of sense
from the hyperactive brain of mine

learning to let go of the fear

a hug

that's what I really want

it's hauntingly in the air

the feeling

I can have a great week

but at the end all I want is hug

the beauty of the earth in my eyes

with the beauty of her hair resting on my shoulder

       cuddled together
       watching the world on fire
       but finding warmth in the heat

    it's at the heart of all I write about

in spring the trees protect me from the rain
       summer, they block the rays
autumn, they color the atmosphere
       winter, they die to give way for cheer

           will they ever love me?

     green
       my favorite color

spend too much of the day in worry, it will leave you lonely

though, worrying about another leaves you smiling
because it means you found something worth the anxiety

Glass Half What

The question at hand,
is how being so full of it,
leaves you so empty in the end.
This is a contradiction of pride.
What's true and what's not,
and who really are you?

For Fuck's Sake

I'm the kid who can't get his head out of a notebook, he just keeps writing and writing, he's lying to himself, says he trying to be himself, why do I feel so lost? Tonight could have been my chance, but I'm screaming, this is hardly singing! Fuck. Why is it so hard to talk, I could go on and on about nonsense that doesn't matter, but I can't tell a friend anything from the heart. I finally know who my real best friend is, this damn pen I keep strapped to my chest! I wrote all these thoughts down, when will I share them? I'm almost home now, another night gone, turn the keys, music's gone, my phone sits quietly, what a shitty feeling to blame yourself. For fuck's sake.

A Broken Clock

A broken clock is right twice a day,
a broken heart is right to say
you won't get by without crying.
Tears let the sadness leave,
but you're wondering why everyone else leaves.
If you look to the clock for hope
you can still be happy for a couple minutes.
A broken clock is right twice a day,
and everything else feels wrong. Stay.
Stay at 10:36 with me.
We'll always have this minute,
a broken clock can still be right,
don't leave, don't leave me please,
because the rest of the time
I just feel broken.

ODIK: Relationships

My parents love me so much they gave me two homes.
Relationships are where the complications hit.
Do best friends really last forever?
Because I hardly know who mine are anymore.
You see, there's another girl I am friends with
and I wonder if she has the same feelings for me.
How do you draw a line
between loneliness and friendliness?
Am I my best friend?
I hope not, I'm annoying as heck.
I'm sure one day I'll know.

Fuck It

I wanna find a girl who will remember the sunset
we saw on our first date. We could just say fuck it
to worrying about tomorrow and be happy tonight.
Would then everything be just right? And even
if it wasn't then we would still have each other
and I would do everything to let her know I love her.

She Hugged Me Tight

My lie and die, from my mind alright,
I can't eat for I don't breath,
for I won't say what I can't believe.
I just wanted a hug on a winter night,
she hugged me tight. Oh, just shine on.
I loved a ladybug she left the earth,
for things only get worse.
I won't love another, for loss is the last thing,
I let you down, it's the thing I feel at all.

She dared me again, this time I gave in.
I didn't know what I was doing,
and hesitated to respond to what she said.
Oh, just shine on. I just want a hug,
and the cactus is the one who gave me one.
That's why I'm sad, I mean I'm not really.
It's just cold outside.

When Life Gives You a Diamond

Take note. When life gives you a diamond, don't fall under the pressure. Live without fear of losing a fight because every winner lost before they won. Diamonds are best worn around your heart.

Write a Poem

Chapter VII: I'm walking outside, it's a bit cloudy today

Rainclouds and thunderstorms are the forecast,
I'm sitting in a coffee shop watching it all.
The rain beats and the wind sings.
I just hope everyone I love is still alive.
Waiting for another call I don't want to have,
and I'm missing the call from the one who
makes my heart hurt less. Sigh.
That's the call that never comes.

Damn Wind

Damn wind hitting my face,
blowing my thoughts across the park.
Opportunity doesn't come in a steady stream,
It rushes in like a roaring wave.
Never felt more alive,
the air in my hair,
a paper capering pen,
the current of life sweepin' in.
Damn wind keeps pushing me thin,
it blows open the door
and I have to pull it shut.
Oh, shit. *Ha-ha*

21st Century

The adults all seem alarmed
by all that's going on,
while we've grown up with this,
this is what we expect.
So, if you're wondering why
the kids are all anxious and sad,
we grew up in the lost cause 21st century.

OKC to New York City

Hop on a train and ride away.
Get out before the collapse.
The thought of a new life sounds so promising
because the record will be made clean.
Will my friends even miss me?
What if I delete all my contacts that aren't mom?
Feel the wind in your hair
as the tears begin to heal.
Live the life of a man unafraid of pain.
See the sights, the lights shining bright.
I'll keep my words, publish them in the big city,
and be a respected writer amongst my peers.
No more of this shaking in faltering fears.
I have enough money to buy a ticket.
Why don't I?

Jacket in the Summer

Silvia, why do you wear your jacket in the summer?
Your makeup takes up the space on your face
where you know you've always been beautiful.
You used to be the light in my life
but now you keep your distance from me.
Silvia, you always carry a black diary
and you won't let the world see inside of it.
You stare out the window,
pale and scared; your beauty stolen from you.
There I am sitting next to you, a world away,
and I don't notice the tear in the corner of your eye.
And for that, I'm so sorry.

hope like a drug

where the light goes it will mislead,
i use my hope like a drug,
a strange sense of optimism indeed.

Sober Up

You get me drunk on my hope,
a fantasy I'll never hold.
But when my mind sobers up,
I call you for the bullshit you really are.

Forgotten and Unloved

I sit forgotten and unloved by the world,
I fall to the ground, filled with doubt.
All hope has departed from me here,
yet I hear your call in the distance
and I know you are near.

Five-Forty

You're driving down life's highway
drunk behind the wheel,
my best friend for-whatever is a moronic idiot.
The kid I once knew took a five-forty turn,
now I'm going to watch as your world burns.
You got what you wanted,
are you happy now?

A Phone Call

I got a call.
He seemed shook, on the verge of tears.
I wasn't the least surprised.
Your parents told me it was on purpose,
you did tell me you hated your life.
It's a good thing you're still alive,
at least I like to think so.
Hope you do too.

Are These Walls Stretching?

You think these walls are stretching?
You're running out of breath.
I think it's simply cozy.
What's life without a little death?

Or Is It Your Imagination?

Let me remind you,
you may be in control on the outside,
but up here, there are no windows and no doors.
All these voices echoing,
telling you each way to turn,
but you know deep down
that there's always my way out.
It's what you want, you know it.

Yellow, Orange, Red

Will the trees ever change to yellow, orange, and red? By winter they'll all be dead. So until then, color the atmosphere with joy. The only thing that would make this evening better, is if instead of texting you, you were right here. I'll enjoy this season as much as I'll miss you and all that could have been. For fuck's sake, I want to not miss out on being me. So, before I drink all of my coffee can I save the world from winter?

I'm scared of another winter like the last. I want to cuddle up in a jacket by a fire, not stand alone in a dark, cold snowstorm. No, not this time. I think I'm a hero, but am I really? Can I save the world from winter? I can't even save myself from my anxiety. I need to learn to embrace it, not hide behind a mask. And maybe I have. After all, this is fall.

The Irony of Hell

Do you remember when you
asked me what Heaven must be like?
You said Hell doesn't scare you,
because why would a loving father
make his daughter live in pain.
The irony completely lost on me.

I'm Just Tired

I'm not even eighteen and three of my friends have tried to kill themselves. I count myself lucky they've all failed so far.

I become desensitized to pain when it's all around me. I once held a girl only to look down and see the cuts and scars. I knew in the moment what she told me would be worsening. I wrote a letter to another; did you get it? My best friend spiraled out of control. Against all odds, I keep standing tall.

I'm tired of seeing texts asking me what I'd do if you tried to kill you. I'm tired of getting told to find you in a hospital. I'm tired of looking in my friends' eyes, hearing them talk, but finding nothing there. I'm just tired.

Scotsville

A girl from Scotsville got an exciting offer,
she would move to the city for her new job.
She knew in this position she could make a difference.
She truly believed kindness would heal us all in time.
So she started packing. She would miss Scotsville.
Before leaving, she volunteered every weekend.
Raised enough money for the schools
that had been so long overlooked.
She remembers what it was like for her as a kid,
struggling just to get by.
God blessed her with a chance to give back.
She hugged her mom and dad tight.
"Don't worry, I'll be back soon," she told them.
They all laughed through the tears.
Scotsville, a hellish place to some, but to her home.
With her whole life ahead of her,
one evening she left that town,
heading to her future in the city.

But at the edge of Scotsville's town limits,
a driver going 75 crashed into her from the side,
and before the paramedics got there, she died.

Happy Stories

There are no happy stories,
just lies.
Lies we tell ourselves to feel like
we deserve to be alive.
Nihilists know there's
no way to live with truth,
if honesty is abused.

Ahh! Blahh! Nahh!

You know what tomorrow is!
Enjoy today, because tomorrow
it all comes crashing down.
Misery upon misery is what my economy is,
I'm a happy elf in a nightmare where I'm the king!
And you know! Ohh! Ahh! Blahh! Nahh!

Lawyers of the Mind

I don't trust therapists. What kind of human profits from other people's misery? They're the lawyers of the mind, the psychos of the psyche.

Invalid Password

I password protected the letter I wrote,
but I can't remember which password it was.
I've tried them all, but they've all failed.
You have the only copy of what I wrote.
Now I can't remember everything I said,
I just know I meant every word.
I hope every word meant something to you,
because the ones you say to me always do.

Miss

What will I miss most once the fireworks die and it's January? I miss the wonder I had when I was younger. How many missed decisions have I made off of hypotheticals? Did I miss the right path because I was looking for a laugh? I've missed many shots, more than I'll ever know. Miss, I'm starting to realize I think more than I show. That's enough! If I keeping fretting about what I'll miss then I'd lose time to smile, and I rather smile at every snowflake falling then the ones melting. But damnit. I miss you.

Failure

At this point I don't even know
if I'm afraid of failure
or just scared of the risk.
What a sad way to live your life.

Shit, people say I lie too much,
but honestly, I'm just afraid of the truth.

Will You Pray With Me?

Dear Lord,
why can things be so sad,
if Jesus died so I can one day be alive?
Mortality doesn't bother me as much as this thought:
If I spend my whole life worrying about shit,
would I have lived anyway?
People wonder how you can love us,
if bad things happen to good people.
I wonder how I can love myself
on the day I realize I'm not a good person.

Lord, I'd be helpless if I was faithless,
but I still don't understand what I'm doing.
If sadness and sorrow are real,
and you don't need faith to see that,
will you at least let me be different?
Let me hold an umbrella for others in the rain,
give them a reason to smile through the pain.
I just want to make someone happy.
Make their a world a little less sad.
Amen.

do you understand yet?

writing isn't about happiness

that's what money is for
and authors don't get paid shit

do you understand yet?

a poet's lament

for the kids who die
from the neglect of love
and the shots of guns

an anxious kid
who's moving out in two weeks
trying to find the courage to love
even if he might leave heartbroken

this is what I'm writing about

faith comes from ink, no?

we write the words we wish were true
and have faith that in time they show us the way

these snippets

they're who I am
and who I am kind of terrifies me

cry

let the sadness leave

tears are refreshing because they
let the sadness leave

thesis

I'm looking for a thesis statement
for my book

do I understand yet?

this is a love story

a falling in love

with the sadness
with the heartbreak

with the doubt
with the uncertainty

with writing

I'm learning it's okay to cry because

I'm learning it's okay to be me

The Weeping of the Childless I

The sky is hazy and faint,
they're gone.
No more can you hear them laugh,
running around without a care.
They're gone.
They spent their last minute screaming,
running around from fear.
They're gone.
What have we done?

Welcome to the land of the free,
where violence is our tyranny.
Suffering is just the price we pay.
The sour taste of grief is known to many
when what we love most is taken;
a life for a rifle and your spare dime.

The Weeping of the Childless II

A mother begging for mercy
and a father begging for forgiveness.
Keep the bullets sounding on the battlefield.
War is fought with blood; don't you get it?
This is our right.
The right to live and the right to die.

Little boy. Little girl.
The backpack you wear is the cross on your back.
Christian fighters don't love you.
Christians only love themselves.
The party of bullets and pro-life signs
is the party winning our churches.
Guns and roses behind the baptismal
because a bunch of white men said it's okay.
Little boy. Little girl. Every day you carry a cross.

The Weeping of the Childless III

She holds a gun in her hand,
thinking about that day again.
She just wants to see her babies again.
Kiss them on the cheek again.
She holds a gun in her hand;
all it took was a few stray bullets.
It was our careless refusal to surrender,
we let a killer on the loose.
She holds a gun in her hand,
knowing she can see them in Heaven.
Why is the world so empty?
Can't she just be happy?!

It's the weeping of the childless,
the sorrow, pain, and bitterness!
The night has never felt this dark.
Tears turn cemetery dirt to mud
and blood-stained clothes are left unwashed.
For tonight will live and love will die.
It's the weeping of the childless,
the pain, the shame, the dying breath.

Seasonal Depression

It's that time of year,
everything feels darker,
everything feels harder.
La-ah, it's seasonal depression,
and every season makes me feel sad.
It's raining, and I'm crying.
It's summer, what a bummer.
It's autumn, and I'm falling down.
It's winter, I feel dead.
La-ah, it's seasonal depression.

A Written Reprise

It's the song you'll never hear.
I never had the courage,
the courage to tell you how I feel.
I sing to myself now a chorus:
You'll never know how pretty I find you,
the time every damn thing you said made me smile,
when you were around every problem went away.
You're not around anymore are you.

Shit, people say I lie too much.
Maybe it's for the best.

Stop Crying

Will you stop crying?
Get yourself together!
This is life!
Oh, why,
why is this life?

Forgotten and Unloved II

I sit forgotten and unloved by the world,
I fall to the ground, filled with doubt.
Yet when I pray for your love,
I know nothing will ever harm me.

No More Rain

Feel the air comin' from the road,
that's what today is about bro.
Nothing's the same,
when there's no more rain,
that causes all this pain.
Today is ours, to oh, gain,
from the rain, that's without pain.

Write a Poem Chapter VII

Chapter VIII: Learning to smile back

The stranger in the hall smiles,
and I don't know how to feel.
The cute girl sitting nearby smiles at me,
and I try my best to smile back.
I smile in the mirror and think what a dork.

Anxious, Impatient

I mumble and stumble,
laugh it off,
keep walking,
keep talking,
you never know when they'll strike,
anxious, impatient,
keep it going,
never stopping,
never going anywhere,
except here.

We Were Kids

We were kids and for some reason I thought those times would never end. I was too busy growing up to see you all doing the same. Now I walk the streets looking at the lights without you guys. Maybe I've got someone new, but the times with you are what I fondly knew. Hey, I guess we all grew up at least.

Banana Pudding

Bitch, you tell me no one will like me.
Well if you keep using language like that,
I wonder why.
You tell me friendship is a risk, I know.
I've lost friends before.
Time is the real bitch.
It's time to fall out of touch.
But no, you try to tell me no one
will care for me the way I do them.
And? It's not like you care about me.
I'd rather put myself out there
and fall flat on my face then never try at all.
So shut up. I don't need you.
I'm not lonely, I just need to be done acting scared.

Honestly, I think you're lonely.
You're the voice trapped in my thoughts,
and you just want to be my friend.
Dude, so do I.

BYHAAA!

You love me.
I love me.
A narcissist in a trench coat.
Heartbreak in a toxic wave.
You love me.
You wish you didn't.
But you let me break your heart again and again.
You don't deserve me,
no one does.
You'll never know how great I am.
And you'll never know what you'd be missing.

Fight or Flight

The lady in the smoking hot dress walks by,
she's the one holding the smoking distress.
Her devilish smile can be felt for a mile,
her whistle is meant for you,
listen to what she says, it's charming you.
Fighting to be free from the alure,
fighting to be free from the very thing.
Keep running.
Keep fighting.
You'll never be free.
Keep running, never dying.
You'll never be free.
Keep fighting, always lying.
Fighting to be free from the very thing,
the very thing you that keeps you running,
running right back to me.

Life Will Be Alright

I was drowning
in a sea of doubts,
that's how the
cliché goes.
My to-do list
kept growing
while the clock
kept ticking.
I'm picking apart
flowers instead
of trying to
grow a garden.
I never know
how the next
day will leave
me standing.

Stop!
Embrace what makes today worth the fight.
Because life will be alright.

Hey kid, sometimes you just need someone to write you a song to remind you life will be alright. What's scaring you today will be tomorrow's strength. So don't get down and out if you can't figure this out. Let's sing and shout and make the most of the day. Take up your fight and just remember, life will be alright.

The Pen, It's a Gateway

In my hand I hold a key,
in my head I have a story,
in my heart is a dream,
and my eyes see the future gleam,
because the pen, it's a gateway.

Keep Writing

Hey, I don't give a damn how good you are.
Kid, you might not win a Pulitzer,
but keep writing if you want. I'm so glad I did.
And I may not be all that good,
but writing gives me a voice
and it lets me tell a story.
So, if it means something to you,
keep writing. You'll get better. (I did)
And if this isn't your thing,
you'll find something that is.
Don't be afraid to find yourself,
because you'll find something great.

Summer's End I

Crispy fruit and ice cream,
it's the same feeling.
You and I playing Mario Kart,
I'll show you all my tricks and dart,
dart right ahead, past Walmart.
Oh! We're driving in the sky.

This Sunday my friend,
we're coming to summer's end,
so until we get to be brothers again,
don't forget to write songs about
how we're driving in the sky!
And y'know, life is our apple pie.

Summer's End II

How's school this year?
Across the street, see those trees
near the park we played on as kids;
whom I kidding,
you still have all of that ahead of you.
You have your friends,
even when summer comes to an end,
you're going to prove 'em all again.
But right now we're driving in the sky,
and life is our apple pie.

That Thing I Forgot To Say

I have the perfect thing to say,
I'll walk straight up and tell you,
but erp, there's a frog in my throat,
and an excuse in my shoulder tote.
So, I won't sing, I'll keep writing,
live to fight another fighting,
I mean, fight to live on keeping,
or keep fighting to fight on living,
you get the point!

Shining Knight

I see myself as a shining knight,
I mean, I've got the charisma,
I won't back down from a fight
with my words as sharp as a sword.
It's time to be my dream hero,
what to do isn't so clear though.
Slaying a dragon is surprisingly hard
when you can't read the map to his lair.
I may see myself as a shining knight,
but in the end, the knight gets the girl,
and I don't.

Stranger In My Head

Tonight went by in a blur, *(for rurl)*
I'm a stranger in my head, *(seeing red)*
living life going through the motions, *(a commotion)*
a contradiction of pride, *(take a side)*
I'm lost where I belong, *(is that wrong)*
living life perfectly out of reach. *(ain't that a peach)*

Twitch

Twitch. Don't talk to me.
Twitch. Don't touch me.

I don't really know what the problem is,
and that's kinda the problem.
I like things organized,
but my mind's a cluttered mess.
Incoherent thoughts,
no time is lost,
afraid of nothing,
and it's the nothingness
that terrifies the most.

Twitch. On the edge.
Twitch. Ready to burst.
Twitch. Sorta scared.
Today was great,
not some better fate.
Twitch. And breathe.

Dentist

Dr. Dandelion, DMD loves her job.
She works to brighten people's smiles.
Ever met someone who has trouble smiling?
They don't realize how beautiful they're happiness is.
Dr. Dandelion holds the hands
of kids afraid of getting teeth pulled,
and then she watches them go away
laughing with a sticker and a smile.
Ever met someone who has trouble smiling?
Dr. Dandelion can turn what you think
is an ugly insecurity into a sparkling grin.
She spent years in dental school
just to watch you be happy again.
Dr. Dandelion, DMD loves her job.
She works to brighten people's smiles.
Ever met someone who has trouble smiling?
She'll help you smile again. Candy or cavities,
she knows smiling makes all of our lives sweeter.

the moment you smiled

the moment I knew

I wouldn't forget this moment

damnit, now I'm back to being a blender

filled with
  hope
  doubt
  laughter
  and anxiety

all mixed together

when you catch me glimpsing your way
and you smile at me

I try to smile back
before you look away again

breathe   that's what we do to live

but breathing is hard
breathe

I'm arrogant
always have been

I'm a white guy in Middle America
things usually work out for me

but for the first time
I don't know if I like the way I look
my hair, it's okay I guess
my clothes are fine
I wish I smiled more

I just don't always like what I see
in the mirror

what does it take to be normal?
I just wanna see the world like everybody else does

when y'all dance in the sun
I pray for clouds
so I can drink coffee and write alone

anxious, impatient
your smile

your damn smile

I've started smiling more

thank you

now when you're around,
all I want to do
is make you smile too

Weather or Not

Whether or not I see you tomorrow,
I'll still be dreaming of the next time I do.
Weather or not, I'll keep this feeling
and the rain overhead won't take that away.
Whether or not I find what I'm looking for,
I'll still be fighting.
Writing to keep the feeling I have.
Weather or not, I know my optimistic thoughts
will echo out the waling wind,
'cuz I don't feel like feeling sad today.
I see dark storm clouds, but I'm the one smiling.
Whether or not, weather or not.

MOORE

Give and Take

Blue clouds over fire skies,
I'll say goodbye. My, this is why.
Why, I remind myself today
isn't the last day of my life.
That sun will rise again when I wake,
and the pain and love each day I give and take.

Gorgeous

For all the pretty ladies that they
called sissies on the playground.
As kids you're teased for being too girly, but when
you grow up you'll never be a women they say.
And it's they who can't keep the story straight.
They're zealous or jealous. But they can't tell us.
Pretty people are pretty,
and honey you're gorgeous.

Hey Little One

Hey little one,
some days it takes courage just to get out of bed
when blankets give more warmth than the world.
Remember, you don't need to slay a dragon
to have an adventure.
It takes confidence just to walk outside.

Hey little one,
some days it takes courage just to smile
when you have doubts about what you're doing.
Remember, you don't need to live a story tale
to find a little joy.
It takes confidence just to be able to feel sad.

Hey little one,
some days it takes courage just to be you.
But we all love it when you do.

Driving Home III

I pray that you'll give me the strength to do my best and every day my best will get better. Through you I can do anything. Through anything I can lead and serve. For this I know I have every reason to sing.

Anxious, Impatient II

Truth is, I'm happy to be here.
Home is nice and cozy,
I have hideaways where everything is rosy,
but stepping outside my doors, won't leave tears.
This smile I have really is real,
I'm anxious, impatient, but laughing too,
I'm no longer afraid of something new.
I'm glad to see you, and that's how I really feel.

A Mirror and You

You and your pretty face,
the way you fill this empty space.
I just think your cute to put it simply,
be it that smile or your sweater.
And it's when I look in the mirror
I wish I looked better.
I have messy hair, crooked glasses,
and this acne and spots peeling at my skin,
but for you it just adds color to your grin.
How does your smile seem so real?
I've been practicing smiling in my mirror
and it always looks forced and stupid.
Yet when you smile at me, I can't help but be happy.
And I just hope I've learned to smile back.

Write a Poem Chapter VIII

Chapter IX: Iced coffee in winter

Snowfall and iced mocha,
things that fall from the sky,
this is why I lie.
I'm stressing over enjoyment,
this holiday will keep me awake,
life a caffeine high.
I'll write on my hand, a reminder to live life.

Pumpkin Spice

It's the time of year of pumpkin spice and everything nice. I dusted off my jacket and my hope again. I love football, pie, and October lies. This crisp breeze bites at you under sepia-hued skies. For the rest of the year I've fallen in love with Autumn air and your beautiful hair. Hey fall, don't let this feeling fall away.

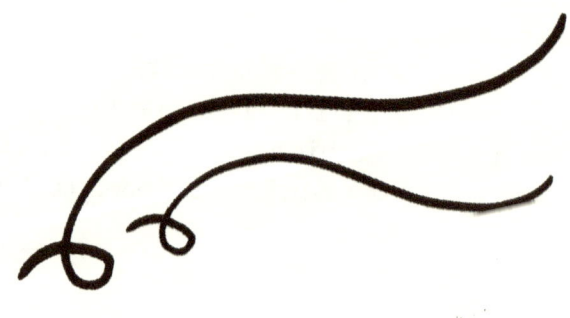

My Last Christmas

I'm not ready for Christmas to pass, because what if it's my last? If I grow up, will all the magic be lost? All I want for Christmas is to sit around the tree. Let the fireplace thaw all the memories for me.

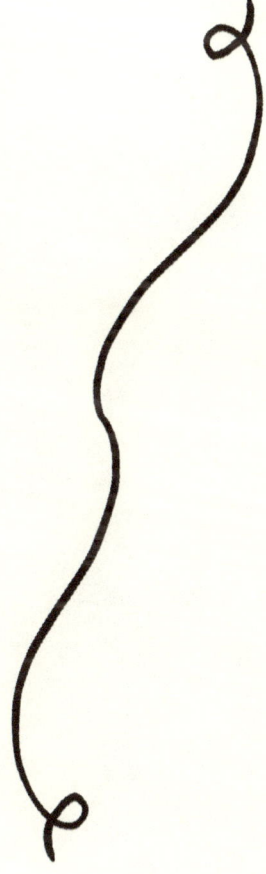

Ghosts on My Computer

I've written a few poems about ghosts,
they're the ones when I reread, it hurts the most.
I kinda want to delete them from my hard drive
but I guess they were still a part of my life.
If I get rid of the ghosts of yesterday
I wouldn't be the person I am today.

I'm a Bit Shaky

I'm a bit shaky,
probably from that coffee,
why are we laughing?
It's sorta funny,
I started talking,
first, I thought,
then I lost it,
but I own it,
phoned it,
I'm here,
they hear,
but where is there?

Write Away

I'm the kinda guy who wonders why he's cold,
when he drives with his windows down in November.
I'll watch the first snowfall with glee, and say I like
the bitter cold because it makes me feel alive.
Why though?
Does everyone try to make
a lifetime out of each day?
Tries to live each day like the year is almost over,
like they know every second is there chance.
I'm the kinda guy who want to be cold, if it means
I can wear a jacket and drink coffee by the fireplace.
I think I can write away my problems tonight.

I'm the kinda guy who wonder why he's lonely,
when he refuses to talk to his friends.
I'll be happy to eat alone, because I know
I'm too anxious to eat around others.
Why though?
Does everyone think their friends
find them an inconvenience?
Tries to live each day like the year will never end,
because they don't know where they're going.
I'm the kinda guy who want to be cold, if it gives
me an excuse to celebrate with friends and family.
I think I can write away my problems tonight.
Now I've gotta find out if I'm right.

True Inspiration

This may be the greatest thing I've ever wrote,
I've never felt inspired to be this honest.
You see, I think I understand the truth of love-
Ooh look, a squirrel!

What was I talking about again?

An Idea

An idea,
it's all you need
to be freed.

Quiet Life

My love lives in the suburbs,
my family dines in the Braum's diner down the street.
Order a pizza or see a movie on the weekend,
hide away in the semi-pretty parks
and the back of the li-berry.
It's the quiet life that I find worth the seek.

Not Perfect

I held a door shut on a windy day and it got me thinking. You'll never hear it, but my first chorus isn't even true anymore. The trouble with my mind is it never stops. Your little white lies, I see you in my rearview mirror. Sometimes I just need you to leave me alone. I want to enjoy this wonderful evening, but I'm worried I'll let it escape by. Because right now I sit alone in my car unsure of where to go. But damn, feel that slight breeze. A paper capering pen with me. I'm sitting under the shady tree, listening to music and it's just me. I know this won't be my best poem, but I won't ever stop loving to write. And this isn't the perfect night, just another day in the perfect life for me.

start with nonsensical screaming

         repeat the same three chords

    sing loud and sing fast

          and you got yourself a punk song

time to drive
         windows down
         music's on
         say a prayer

dear God,
thank you for today
this beautiful day will be inspiration for me
       (it doesn't matter the weather)

        I don't write because it'll make me popular
          haha, I'm embarrassed each time
          I tell someone I like to write
          they always ask me what and I gulp
          before saying poems and songs

no, I write because I'm inspired to do so

        love and trees
        faith and family
        hope and despair
        art

I want to learn to play guitar

I'm determined to finally let
people hear what I have to say

I want to write a book

I'm determined to be me

I've been creating things for years

board games out of cardstock paper
episodical sci-fi masterpieces (the first 3 chapters anyway)
an awesome kata and cat-themed kata jokes (cat-a, get it)
worlds in my mind, words in the sky

I'm singing in my car

I'm dreaming of being in love

I'm inspired to inspire
I've inspired myself to respire
respiring till I'm finally alive

you know what to do

scream, sing loud, sing fast
uaagggh! let's go!

this is my art...my life

Caffeine High

My mind is always on a caffeine high,
thinking faster than I can think of thinking,
mocha-induced sweetness on my breath,
when everything around me is beautiful,
the world is lovely if you look at the right time,
and each day I'll capture what makes it so,
because it's my choice to love life,
I'm a bit shaky, a bit achy, a bit flaky, a bit turned around,
I'm the one with pen, I'll be your best friend,
and we can enjoy the beauty we create around us,
up until day's end.

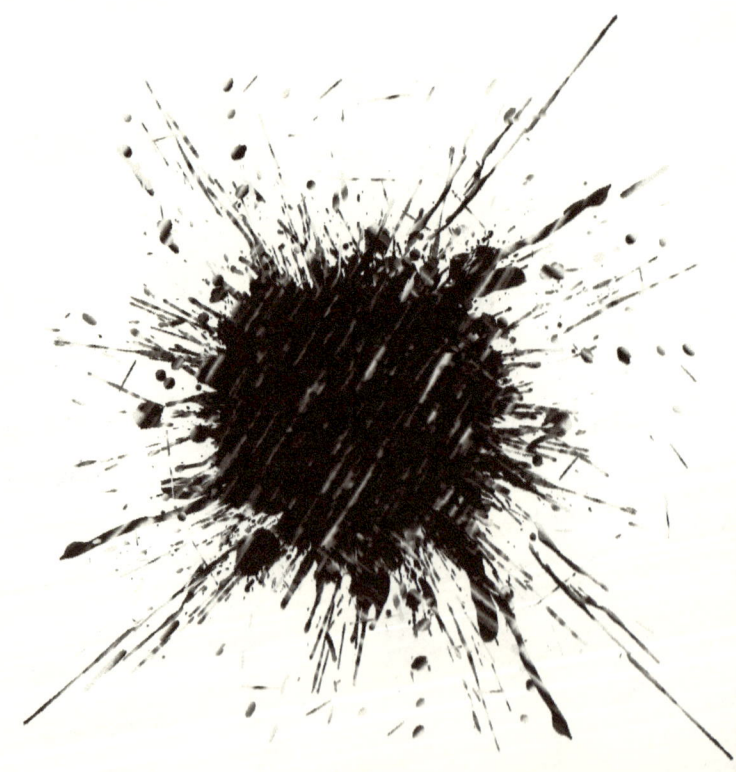

Grab Coffee With Me

Will you grab coffee with me?
Laugh the night away,
too caffeinated to sleep.
Just the few of us,
talking and being kids.
Will you grab coffee with me?
Talk like we're best friends again,
without life getting in the way.
How's it going, I think about you y'know.
You get my jokes, I get your struggle,
because a part of you has rubbed off on me.
Will you grab coffee with me?
We can get to know each other better,
I can look in your eyes and feel that gut punch
of anxious excitement as I hear you laugh.
The same feeling I get from this
liquid sugar I'm drinking.
And in this coffee shop is my chance to
tell you how pretty your stupid face is.
Will you grab coffee with me?

Ice in My Life

I need ice in my life
and snow in my soul.
Give me a reason to go slow.
I need fire in my heart
and sunlight in my eyes.
Give me a reason to be brave.
I need the wind in my hair
and rain on my coat.
Give me a reason to keep fighting.

Don't Say a Thing

Don't you say a thing,
this is problem you can't fix.
Just be there. Just listen.
Not every problem has an answer.
Don't you say a thing.
Just be there. Just listen.
Just say you love me,
no matter the pain I'm going through.

Believe in Me

Silvia asked me if God is real,
then why did he forget about her.
Heaven is like that distant dream,
a fantasy of make-believe.
She said, "Why would I believe in God,
if he doesn't believe in me?"

Peppermint and Chocolate

Every year the taste of peppermint and chocolate rushes in the holiday spirit. But right now, all I can do is think about a girl that I let go to soon because the truth made me fear it. I can't stop wishing your head was on my shoulder. As the cold December breeze fills the air, I would give my jacket to hold her. Anymore it's dark out and I sit alone in my car drinking my shake, looking to the right. I still remember when you were sitting next to me in the passenger seat, but now memories are all I have of that night.

memories

memories are the mind's greatest lie,
moments that no longer exist
left there just to remind you to cry.

By My Side

I try to remind myself to look to the right,
not because of some past night,
but because I know you're always by my side.
I know deep in my heart there's no better comfort,
than your hand on my shoulder, always nearby.
I won't have to be in life alone, cause you're my hope.

Hymnal

A comfort so familiar,
from music.
That anxious pit in my stomach,
the labyrinth in my mind,
will be soothed in music.
Sitting on the edge,
the senses of what's senseless,
lifting up a voice in confidence,
trying to understand the music.

How Do You Write a Love Song?

How do you write a love song? I'm trying to figure out how I can take the romance of fall and spell it out. I'm trying to figure out how I can find a girl who will love me. Or actually, am I trying to find a girl I can love? I wanna know what's it like to write a song, find a bench under the sunset-schemed-trees, and sing it the one and only person I wrote it for. She's the only canvas more lovely than the one staring out my window. I'm a poet, it's time for me to show it.

I Wanna Know

I wanna know what it's like to live, and to laugh,
and to find a girl to fall in love with.
I wanna know what it's like to write a song,
and to play guitar and sing along.
I wanna know what it's like to feel like me
and to spend my time where I want to be.

Quietly Falling

I'm quietly falling in love.
Falling in love with life,
the beauty of art and majesty of earth,
falling in love with you, in thought at least.
I'm quietly falling in love,
oh, quietly wondering.
Wondering why the world is such a show;
we show others we're in love,
can I show myself I'm in love?
I'm quietly alone, and that's okay.
I'm drinking my coffee,
calmed by all the books in the library.
I'm not on the party scene or social media,
instead I'm teaching myself to breathe,
so when I'm around friends I don't panic.
I'm quietly falling in love.
Falling in love with life,
the beauty of art and majesty of earth,
I'll fall in love with you if I don't let myself down.
I want to fall... I want to shout...
I want to know what love is about.
I'm quietly falling in love.

Watching

I'm sitting in the library hall, watching Heaven's tears drip down Oklahoma oaks, while I write alone in a notebook with an annoyed look on my face.

Ver la Luna

Oh, bebe no te vayas,
esta noche esperemos, podemos ver la luna,
sin ti la alegría de la noche no es ninguna.
Te vas a reir,
yo amaré.
Oh, bebe no te vayas,
esta noche esperemos, podemos ver la luna,
sin ti la alegría de la noche no es ninguna.
Sabes que te amo,
¿tú también me amarás?

Write a Poem Chapter IX

Chapter X: I tried taping together the pieces of my pen, I think it worked

Snippets. Just a peak at the ink spilled.
Tape doesn't hold for long, it's chaotic.
I'm scared of it, that's why I love it.
I can't finish this, think about it.
If this it, well, what's next?
I've got my pen. I've got my friends.
I'll learn to just roll with it.

Old Glasses

I can't see through these glasses,
what is life when love is blurred.
Everything is out of focus,
it all looks like hocus pocus.
I feel removed when I rely on a broken lens,
all I want is to pull close my friends.

Ink, Paper, Scissors

Ink, paper, scissors, shoot.
I've been using the same pen all year,
Uni-Ball Signo 207. It's a black pen with a clicker.
I write things out or type them up.
The ink spreads on the paper.
One of my students asked me why I like poetry,
I told him words are like building blocks,
and if you use them right
you can make something beautiful.
I keep a drawer in my dresser with office supplies,
I print my words and use scissors to cut them out.
I dreamed of writing a book;
to play a game of ink, paper, scissors. Shoot.

The Blue Summer Notebook Remix

You think you're a writer? Prove it.
Think you can sing, when you don't know music.
Hey kid, who knows shit.
Bring a notebook and find out.

I brought a blue notebook with me that summer,
I would write each word 'till it made a melody.
I can write, but I can't sing,
and that ain't gonna stop me.
So, listen up. These words gave me my start.
That walk in July when I saw my little brother,
I was lost in thought he was right where he was,
hey baby brother, what's going on in your mind?
I had a crush on this girl, so I wrote a song.
It's the song you'll never hear
because fuck that shit.
The damn wind pushes me thin,
but I've got my pen and boy, am I good at lies.
Those little white lies. The ghost in your mirror.
So, listen up. About time to act like it,
you think that's fucking wrong? Guess what,
I've been swearing since my first song.
Love thy neighbor as yourself.
Is that drowning in your fears?
If so, you can kiss my tears.
It was the blue notebook that gave me my start,
the six songs I first thought of.
You think you're a writer?
Well here's the proof.

Trinkets and Doodads

I am a vagabond. I go town to town selling trinkets and doodads. I love this life. Every day, I can see new places with new people. For a moment every day I can be a part of someone else's life. Whether I make a difference or just get a chance to see a snippet of what their life looks like, I find myself smiling by the end of everyday just thinking about all the people around me with their own unique stories.

X: I tried taping together the pieces of my pen, I think it
worked | 324

When Life Pushes Me Over

With your words piercing the air,
I know I'll never be lost.
When night brings dark thoughts,
I know you'll protect and care.

When life knocks me over, I'll stand back up.
When life pushes me down, I'll stand back up.
When I have no legs left to walk on,
you will carry me upon your shoulder.

Maturing

Every week I feel wiser and taller. I didn't want to mature but was forced to. I'm a better person now, but I don't always know if I'm a happier one.

A Hero's Legend

Paragon's legend grew and grew,
all he needed was an opposite.
Only where the dark consumes,
can a light thrive, and a hero die.
A light in the darkness,
a paragon of love for another,
a hero like none other.

New Friends

New friends,
new memories,
someone I knew,
is now gone,
but they're right here too,
relative to the night,
nothing is right,
but in life, tonight,
is what I'll want,
so I thought,
but this is what I got.
Huh.

Talk in Rhymes

I've begun to talk in rhymes, speaking the music notes in my mind. I've begun to talk from the heart, and I don't know if that's a good thing. I mean probably; I still can't realize that being me is okay. I think others think I'm an inconvenience. When I talk to friends, there's that lingering guilt in my voice. Like, why should I be bothering you? I act confident, and sometimes I am, but no one is as confident as that voice in my head. That's why when I write it's from the heart. Honestly; that's who I want to say I am.

A Deafening Song

They'll give a pen to anyone nowadays,
so now I'm stuck writing on this paper.
I'm the only one listening, with nothing to be proud,
not allowed, an offbeat singer crying out loud,
he's crying for some attention,
he sings with emotion, an imperfection,
the sound he makes a deafening infection.
Rhyming to hide his lack of musical talent
and screaming just to feel something again.

Here We Are

You keep me thinking,
of all my thoughts,
the one's with you are the best.
I don't think of memories and hope as the enemy
if it means your there just as well.

I'm trying to finish this song,
this is the time I'll tell you about how I feel,
you and I together is what I keep dreaming,
so under the light of the night, here we are.

X: I tried taping together the pieces of my pen, I think it
worked | 332

Another Typewriter

CLICK
I design my own world,
filled with my own words.
It's a beautiful place where everything is just right,
it's so nice. Where I'm the damn hero,
a self-published story of the creator,
who finds a way to connect with everyone,
teach everyone what's it like to be today's best,
has a way of making his friends smile,
and his girl fall in love time and time again.
I'm still a little anxious to write fiction,
not as much as I once was though.
CLICK
I design my own world,
filled with my own words.
And it's the world I'm living in,
making the most of who I am,
and the I am I will be next.
CLICK

Award Season I

When all is said and done, there's only so many days left in the year. It's up to me now to make time for what I love. I'll enjoy the holiday and not worry about next year, ha, not yet anyway. Tears, wonders, fears, ponders. Heartbreak hurts so much, but it's not the wins that make me who I am, but the losses. When it's time to make resolutions, I can smile knowing this year I came out battered and bruised, but still on top.

Award Season II

And the award goes to... you!
You made it.
You made us proud.
For every hit that knocked you down,
every tear that hit the ground,
you made it.

Christmas Time Again

Oh, it's Christmas time again!
It doesn't matter that the air's cold,
'cuz the fire's warm and our hearts gold.
Oh, it's Christmas time again!
It's Christmas time again!
Jingle bells rock and I get out all my favorite socks,
there's this season to find a reason for love.
Because when we gather around the tree,
we're smiling with friends and family.
Oh, it's Christmas time again!
It's Christmas time again!

X: I tried taping together the pieces of my pen, I think it
worked | 338

Fireworks Lit the Sky

On the Fourth of July
the explosions shouted around us.
We all jumped in our excitement,
yet you didn't even bat your sleepy little eyes.
Fireworks lit the sky,
dreams soared as you lied.

Love Never Left

Ferme les yeux mon enfant,
rêve de demain,
ne perds pas espoir,
l'amour n'est jamais parti.

X: I tried taping together the pieces of my pen, I think it

Sunset-lit Skies

I'll save the best for last,
and wait for the perfect moment,
like a slight breeze in a sunset-lit sky,
but this ain't my perfect world,
and if you wait until the end,
chances are it'll never come.

Shine

Goodnight sun,
I hope you know what it's like to get a night of sleep.
You're so bright and cheery,
all you do is love.
When you leave I don't frown,
because I'll see you in the morning.
You never stop shining,
you never tire, no matter the heartache,
all you do is love. You're always there.
Goodnight sun.

Writer's Sock

I wear socks under my shoes
and fear under these words.
Mismatch stockings,
remix poetry.
This book isn't life advice
or some great story.
It's just a bunch of ramblings.
I like cute socks with
narwhals wrapped in Christmas lights.
This book is just a bunch of thoughts,
something I have too much of.
A taped-together art project,
shreds of brilliance and scribbles of nonsense.
It's not some great story,
but it's my story.

A Conversation With Izzy

"Can you send me a copy of that?" I asked.

 "Sure, here you go." she said.

"Great, I just got it."

"This is pretty good. No wonder you're the writing major and I'm the college dropout."

 "Nah, you're a good writer too."

"Ehh, sometimes. I think I'm a great writer, but I'm also convinced I'm the only one who thinks that."

 "Well even I don't think I'm any good."

"And I think no one likes me and my friends all secretly think I'm super annoying."

 "Yeah, totally. I think you're very annoying."

"Oh, I know. Haha, don't you love being anxious all the time?"

 "Oh, of course. It's the best."

"I guess I just wish I smiled more."

 "You should, you have a nice smile. Everyone tends to thinks I hate them; and my smile does looks fake."

"Well, they're the ones wrong then. You're one of the kindest people I know.

 "Thank you. I just think people should be treated with love, you know, no matter their sex, race, or if they're gay. Sounds crazy, right?"

"Yeah what kind of liberal BS are you talking about? Treating people nicely, that's absurd."

 "Sure seems that way sometimes."

the pieces of the pen on my desk

I wrote something
I hope you love it

when the world is screaming
love, when there's nothing left but to die

we'll hold the candle
burn the world

our words the only thing

remaining

I'm lost
alone

finding

happiness
contentment
friendship   finding myself

do you need a hug?

it's cloudy outside
it's raining inside of us

crying to let the sadness leave
it's okay to not be okay
it's okay to be alive

I need a hug

                    I need to hug someone

find someone to love

                    I love you mom
to give my jacket to   *I love you dad*
  (my love,   *I love my brothers,*
     you don't need to cover the cuts)   *my sisters*
                              I love my friends,
to hold their hand   *my family*
        to see them smile

                    I've been trying to smile

        I've been smiling more
                overcoming anxiety more
                mostly embracing it more

I know what's true to me
        I'll love you so you don't have to be alone
                              with the sadness
            I want to love you
                I want you to love me
                              don't we all

it's windy and cold, just the way I like it
        have you ever heard a tree speak?

they're alive   they speak of art

        let's take part

what is life?

                    the beauty of light
                    in the darkness

        respiration is my inspiration

    the pieces of the pen taped together is a mess,
      the mess of ink bound together is my life.

Driving Home IV

I take the long way home, the path with all the scenery. I drive past the trees, the lake, and field of dandelion weeds. I want to say thank you for the wonderful life around me. You gave me your word and I'll smile every day knowing it.

X: I tried taping together the pieces of my pen, I think it
worked | 348

Sentimental Value

I had this pen I was using to write all of my poems, but I lost it last week. It's not like I don't have other pens that are the exact same, I'm using one right now. No, the pen just had sentimental value. I used it to write my first books and they're almost done now, just a few more edits. I was going to retire that pen once I finished, but I lost it. I hope if someone finds it they write something great with what little ink was left. I know I'll keep writing at least.

Maturing II

I try to not regret anything because the past made me, me. But I'm still learning to let go of it. I was raised on fairy tales and happy endings, but I wasn't ready for the story to never end. I'm a writer because that's when I get to control the narrative. Life is mine, but there's no autocorrect. It's like I said, music is my therapy.

Have You Ever

Have you ever wrote so much
the ink in your pen ran out,
the pages in your notebook fell out?
Have you ever been so glad you couldn't speak,
so mad you felt meek,
so sad you felt weak?
Have you ever lived just to not die?
Have you ever been in love,
so much in love you still remember to love yourself?
Have you ever sung so loud you lost your voice,
with enough passion to lose the choice
to keep this to yourself?
Words aren't real,
that's what makes them so powerful.
Have you ever realized the truth in them,
the truth in your words,
and the truth in who you are?

Have you ever...

Stained II

The page is still stained.
It's a mess, it's incoherent, it's art.
The letters fall from my mind,
until they make words. They make a story.
I've taken a hit, so I'll strike right back.
Roll with the punches, fight till I drop.
Bloody these knuckles and embrace the pain,
my blood will mix with the ink spilt.
The emotion soaks in.
The hope of what I've said,
it makes me smile at who I've become.
I'll fall in love day and day again.
I won't write without breathing, believing,
embracing every anxiety and thought in my mind,
the spill of ink a mess, a perfection.

Snippets of Ink
By Joshua Crocker

Write a Poem Chapter X

Index

Acknowledgements

Thank you to my family: my mom, my dad, Samantha, Caleb, Kaylee, Thomas, Ali, Kevin, my grandparents, my aunts and uncles, and my cousins. I love each one of you.

Thank you to the family I've got to create; the people who I can always count on, and I love to be around. I hope each one of you finds a way to express what makes you so awesome. Thank you to Isabella and Kayla for agreeing to read, review, and help edit my first two books. I'm grateful to have other people to give me an extra perspective on the words I've written.

Thank you to the people who helped me realize who I am. The people who taught me how to stand up for what you believe in, treat others with love, and be happy with who you are.

And thank you to the pen I always carry with me. You always seem to have just enough ink to write something great. I can't wait to open my notebook to the next page and write something new.

About the Author *circa 2023*

Joshua is a freelance writer, martial arts instructor, and media lead. He has a black belt in integrated martial arts, having spent over two-thirds of his life training. As of this time, he has written over 40 full-length poems/songs and 2 books. He is working on creating a coalition of local writers and creators. He hopes to give others a chance to tell their story to the world and themselves.

Snippets of Ink is Joshua's second poetry collection. Following *One Day I'll Know*, a collection of longer poem/songs, Snippets of Ink takes a different direction. Like spilled ink all over the place, the book's shorter form of poetry includes excerpts from Joshua's other works and an assorted collection of short poems.

All photos in Snippets of Ink were taken by Joshua on his phone. Each picture is from around his hometown of Moore and Norman, Oklahoma.

"The ink splashes on the page because my art, it's a getaway. My thoughts become words because the pen, it's a gateway."

- Joshua Crocker